The Anxious Woman's Mind

The Evidence-Based Guide to Breaking the Anxiety Cycle, Calming Hormonal Anxiety, Releasing People-Pleasing, and Building Genuine Calm

Alex Z. Morgan

Vitality Press

Copyright

First published 2025. Printed in the United States of America.

Disclaimer

This book is written for educational and informational purposes only and is not intended as a substitute for professional medical or psychological advice, diagnosis, or treatment. The techniques and approaches described are drawn from clinically validated research but are not a replacement for working with a qualified mental health professional. If you are experiencing severe anxiety, depression, or any other mental health condition, please seek professional help. The author and publisher expressly disclaim any liability for any adverse effects arising from the use of information contained in this book.

Table of Contents

INTRODUCTION

Why Anxiety Hits Women Harder — And What to Do About It

Anxiety is the most common mental health condition in the world. And women experience it at nearly twice the rate of men.

This is not a coincidence. It is not a sign of weakness. And it is not simply because women are more willing to talk about their feelings, as the outdated explanation would have it. The higher rates of anxiety in women are driven by a combination of biological, psychological, and social factors that are specific to female experience — factors that most anxiety books, written for a general audience, never address.

Fluctuating estrogen and progesterone directly affect the brain's fear response and threat-detection systems. Women are socialized from childhood to prioritize the emotional needs of others over their own, creating a chronic internal conflict between self and role that is one of the most reliable anxiety generators known to psychology. Women face a unique combination of social expectations — to be competent and accomplished but not threatening, to be warm and available but also professional, to be mothers and partners and employees and friends simultaneously — that creates a level of cognitive and emotional demand that would tax any nervous system.

The result is a particular kind of anxiety that is not fully captured by general anxiety frameworks. It is anxious attunement to others — a constant scanning of the emotional environment for signs of disapproval, conflict, or unmet needs. It is the worry about worry itself — the self-critical overlay that turns ordinary anxious thoughts into something more shameful and harder to address. It is the physical component — the hormonal swings that make anxiety feel different and more intense at specific points in the menstrual cycle, in the postpartum period, and in perimenopause. And it is the exhaustion that comes from managing all of it while meeting the demands of a life that does not slow down to accommodate a nervous system under pressure.

This book addresses all of it. Not anxiety in general — anxiety as it is experienced by women, with all the specificity that requires.

The Gap in Anxiety Resources

Walk into any bookstore and you will find dozens of books on anxiety. Many of them are excellent. Most of them are written for a general audience — human beings who experience anxiety, without attention to the ways in which anxiety is shaped by gender, by hormones, by social role, by the specific psychology of women's development.

This gap has consequences. A woman who reads a general anxiety book and learns that the solution to her anxiety involves asserting her needs more clearly, reducing people-pleasing, and prioritizing her own well-being may find the advice accurate but still struggle to implement it — because the book has not addressed why those things are so much harder for women than the advice implies, and has not given her the specific tools that her specific situation requires.

Understanding the female anxiety landscape — the hormonal, relational, and social dimensions that shape how anxiety manifests in women — is not just interesting background. It is practically necessary for effective treatment. When you know that your premenstrual anxiety spike is partly a hormonal event, you can respond to it differently. When you understand that your people-pleasing is an anxiety management strategy rather than a character trait, you can address the anxiety rather than just trying harder to be more assertive. When you recognize that the maternal anxiety you experience is common and treatable rather than a sign of inadequate mothering, the shame that amplifies the anxiety diminishes.

What This Book Is and Is Not

This is an evidence-based guide. Every technique and framework in this book is drawn from clinically validated research — primarily from Cognitive Behavioral Therapy and Acceptance and Commitment Therapy, the two most extensively studied psychological approaches to anxiety — supplemented by research in neuroscience, endocrinology, and attachment theory.

This is not a book of affirmations or generic wellness advice. It does not tell you to breathe deeply and think positive thoughts. It does not suggest that anxiety is simply a mindset problem you can resolve by choosing differently. It takes anxiety seriously as what it actually is: a physiological and psychological state with real causes and real, evidence-based solutions.

This book is also not a replacement for professional mental health care. If you are experiencing severe anxiety, panic disorder, PTSD, or any condition that significantly impairs your daily functioning, please work with a qualified mental health professional. What this book offers is the educational foundation and practical tools that can complement professional support — or that can address the milder to moderate anxiety that most women experience and that does not always rise to the level requiring clinical intervention.

How to Use This Book

You can read this book straight through, or you can go directly to the chapters that address your most pressing concerns. Each chapter is designed to stand alone while contributing to the larger framework. The exercises at the end of each chapter are practical, not theoretical — they are designed to be done, not just read.

You will get the most from this book if you read it with a journal nearby. Many of the exercises involve writing, and the act of putting thoughts on paper is itself a clinically validated anxiety-reduction technique. Do not worry about doing it perfectly. The point is to engage with the material, not to produce a perfect document.

The chapters follow a logical progression — from understanding the biology and psychology of female anxiety through the specific patterns most common in women, to the tools for addressing them and the lifestyle foundations for lasting change. But if you are in the middle of a specific anxiety challenge right now — a premenstrual week, a postpartum period, a difficult relationship situation — go to the relevant chapter first and return to the beginning when you have the space.

Exercise: Your Anxiety Profile

Before beginning Chapter 1, take 10 minutes to write answers to these questions: (1) When does your anxiety feel worst — morning, evening, before social events, at work, in relationships? (2) What are your three most common anxious thoughts? (3) What does anxiety feel like in your body — where do you feel it? (4) What has helped, even temporarily, in the past? (5) What do you most want to change about how anxiety affects your life? This profile will help you use the chapters most relevant to your experience and will serve as a baseline to compare against when you revisit it in 30 days.

The Shame That Surrounds Women's Anxiety

There is a particular shame that accompanies anxiety in women — a layer of suffering on top of the anxiety itself — that deserves direct attention. Women are expected, culturally, to manage the emotional demands of life: to be the family's emotional regulator, the social connector, the one who notices and addresses others' needs. Experiencing anxiety in this role can feel like a fundamental failure of the expectation.

The shame compounds the anxiety through a well-understood mechanism: shame activates the threat system, which increases anxiety, which increases the shame of experiencing anxiety, in a self-amplifying loop. Women who feel ashamed of their anxiety are less likely to seek help for it, less likely to talk about it with others, and more likely to manage it through avoidance and concealment — behaviors that maintain anxiety rather than reducing it.

One of the most important things this book can do is provide the information that makes shame harder to sustain: the data on how common anxiety is in women, the research on the specific biological and social factors that make it more likely, and the understanding that anxiety is not a character failure but a system response to real pressures. Anxiety in women is not a sign of weakness — it is a comprehensible response to circumstances that genuinely demand a great deal of the nervous system.

A Note on Seeking Professional Support

This book is designed to be practically useful for the range of anxiety that most women experience — from the background hum of chronic worry to the more acute anxiety that accompanies specific circumstances or life stages. It reflects the current evidence base and provides tools that work.

It is not, however, a replacement for professional mental health care when professional care is what is needed. The indicators that professional support is warranted include: anxiety that significantly impairs your ability to function in daily life; panic disorder with recurrent panic attacks; post-traumatic stress disorder; anxiety accompanied by significant depression; anxiety so severe that you cannot engage with the tools in this book; or any anxiety that feels beyond what self-help approaches can address.

Seeking professional help for anxiety is not a failure to handle your own life. It is the appropriate response to a real condition that has effective treatments — and it is an act of self-care that the women in your life benefit from as much as you do. The stigma around mental health treatment is diminishing, and the access to effective care — through in-person therapy, telehealth, and evidence-based self-help programs — is greater than it has ever been. If this book points you toward professional support, that is a success, not a limitation.

Key Takeaways

- Women experience anxiety at nearly twice the rate of men, driven by biological, psychological, and social factors specific to female experience.
- General anxiety frameworks often miss the hormonal, relational, and social dimensions that shape how anxiety manifests in women.
- This book addresses anxiety as women actually experience it — with evidence-based tools drawn from CBT, ACT, neuroscience, and attachment research.
- Every chapter includes practical exercises designed to be applied immediately, not just read.

CHAPTER 1

Understanding the Female Anxiety Cycle

Before you can change an anxiety pattern, you need to understand how it works. Anxiety is not random. It is not a character flaw. It is a system — one that evolved to protect you, that is extraordinarily good at its job, and that in the modern world tends to be significantly over-activated.

Understanding how that system works — and why it is particularly reactive in women — is the foundation of every technique in this book.

The Threat-Detection System

At the center of the anxiety system is the amygdala, a small almond-shaped structure in the brain that functions as the body's threat detector. When the amygdala perceives a threat — whether real or imagined, physical or social — it triggers the stress response: a cascade of hormones including cortisol and adrenaline that prepare the body to fight, flee, or freeze.

This system evolved for physical threats. When a predator appeared, the stress response flooded the body with energy, sharpened attention, and prepared muscles for explosive action. The threat was immediate, the response was immediate, and when the threat passed, the body returned to baseline.

The modern anxiety problem is that the same system activates in response to social threats, future-oriented worries, and abstract concerns — situations where the fight-or-flight response is not only unhelpful but actively counterproductive. When you are anxious about a presentation at work, or worried about a difficult conversation with a friend, or lying awake at 3 a.m. running through everything that could go wrong, the same stress hormones that were designed to help you outrun a predator are flooding your system with no physical outlet.

The consequences of this mismatch are significant. Chronically elevated cortisol damages the hippocampus — the brain structure responsible for contextualizing memory and distinguishing past threats from present reality. It suppresses immune function, disrupts digestion, and impairs the prefrontal cortex's ability to regulate the amygdala — creating a vicious cycle in which chronic anxiety makes the brain less capable of managing anxiety.

Why Women's Threat-Detection Systems Are More Sensitive

Research consistently shows that women have more reactive amygdalae than men — they respond more quickly and more intensely to threatening stimuli. This is not a weakness. It appears to be an evolutionary adaptation related to caregiving: the survival of offspring in early human environments depended on caregivers who were exquisitely attuned to danger and who responded to threats quickly.

This heightened sensitivity extends to social threats. Women's brains are more responsive to social cues — facial expressions, tone of voice, interpersonal dynamics — than men's brains on average. This is the neurological basis for what is often called women's intuition: an above-average ability to read social environments. But in an anxiety context, it also means a greater tendency to detect potential social threats, to ruminate on interpersonal interactions, and to worry about others' perceptions and responses.

Estrogen amplifies this effect. During phases of the menstrual cycle when estrogen is high, amygdala reactivity increases. During the premenstrual phase when estrogen drops sharply, anxiety often spikes. Understanding this hormonal dimension of anxiety is addressed in depth in Chapter 2.

The social dimension adds another layer. Women who have been socialized to be attuned to others' emotional states — which in most cultures includes most women — have developed what researchers call *hypervigilant social monitoring*: a near-constant scanning of the interpersonal environment for signals of disapproval, conflict, or unmet need. This monitoring is protective in environments where women's safety genuinely depends on accurate social reading. But in most modern contexts, it represents an enormous ongoing drain on cognitive and emotional resources.

The Anxiety Maintenance Cycle

Anxiety does not just arrive and leave. It maintains itself through a set of behavioral and cognitive patterns that, paradoxically, are designed to reduce anxiety in the short term but perpetuate it over the long term.

Avoidance is the most powerful of these patterns. Avoiding a situation that triggers anxiety brings immediate relief, and that relief is precisely what teaches the brain the situation was genuinely dangerous. Because avoidance does more than any other pattern to narrow a life, it is examined in detail later in this chapter.

Safety behaviors work similarly. Checking behavior, reassurance-seeking, over-preparation, and people-pleasing are all forms of safety behavior — actions taken to reduce anxiety in the moment that reinforce the underlying belief that the situation is dangerous and that you cannot handle it without these protective measures.

Rumination is the cognitive version of safety behavior. Turning a worry over repeatedly in your mind creates the illusion of problem-solving while actually amplifying the anxious state. The brain interprets the repeated return to a worrying thought as evidence that the thought is important and the situation is dangerous.

The Anxious Body: Physical Symptoms and Their Meaning

Anxiety is as much a physical experience as a cognitive one, and many women are not fully aware of how anxiety is expressed in their bodies. The physical symptoms of anxiety include: heart pounding or racing, chest tightness, shortness of breath, muscle tension (particularly in the shoulders, neck, and jaw), stomach distress, nausea, headaches, dizziness, and fatigue.

For women, the physical symptoms of anxiety are sometimes mistaken for physical illness — because they overlap with symptoms of a range of medical conditions, and because women's physical symptoms are more likely than men's to be attributed to anxiety by healthcare providers, sometimes correctly and sometimes incorrectly. It is important to have physical symptoms evaluated medically before attributing them to anxiety, particularly if they are new, severe, or worsening.

When physical symptoms are indeed anxiety-driven, understanding them as anxiety is itself therapeutic. The heart pounding is adrenaline, not a cardiac event. The stomach distress is the gut-brain axis responding to stress hormones, not a gastrointestinal illness. Knowing this does not make the symptoms disappear, but it removes the secondary anxiety — the anxiety about the symptoms — that amplifies the original experience.

The Role of Avoidance in Maintaining Anxiety

Of all the behaviors that maintain anxiety, avoidance is the most powerful and the most insidious. It is insidious precisely because it works. When you avoid a situation that triggers anxiety, the anxiety drops immediately and significantly. This immediate relief is powerfully reinforcing — it teaches the brain that avoidance is the correct response to the anxiety-triggering situation, and it strengthens the avoidance behavior for next time.

The problem is the long-term cost. Every time you avoid a situation, you confirm to the brain that the situation was genuinely dangerous — that the anxiety was appropriate and the avoidance was necessary. The threat assessment that produced the anxiety is validated rather than updated. And the range of situations that feel dangerous tends to expand over time, as avoidance generalizes from the original trigger to situations that share some characteristics with it.

This is how anxiety grows. Not through dramatic escalation but through the gradual accumulation of avoided situations, each reasonable on its own, that together increasingly constrain a life. The person who avoids one difficult conversation finds that direct communication feels impossible. The person who avoids one social event finds that social engagement feels unbearable. The person who avoids one professional challenge finds that her career has contracted around what feels safe.

The Path Forward

The path out of anxiety maintenance is approach — the deliberate, graduated exposure to anxiety-triggering situations that teaches the brain, through experience, that the situations are manageable. This does not mean plunging into the most frightening situations immediately. It means systematic, supported exposure that allows the brain's threat assessment to update in response to new evidence.

Approach is supported by the cognitive and somatic tools in this book — the techniques that make it possible to enter anxiety-triggering situations without being overwhelmed by the anxiety they generate. The tools do not eliminate the anxiety of approach. They make the anxiety bearable, which is all that is required for the approach to do its work.

Exercise: Map Your Anxiety Cycle

Choose one recurring anxious situation from your profile in the Introduction. Draw a simple cycle: (1) Trigger — what happens? (2) Anxious thoughts — exactly what does your mind say? (3) Physical sensations — where do you feel it in your body? (4) Behavior — what do you do when anxious? (5) Short-term result — relief or avoidance? (6) Long-term consequence — does the anxiety shrink or grow? Identifying your specific cycle makes the intervention points visible. Which step in the cycle do you think is most accessible to change first?

Recognizing Your Anxiety Triggers

Every person's anxiety has a signature set of triggers — the specific situations, thoughts, or physical states that reliably activate the threat-detection system. Knowing your triggers does not eliminate them, but it transforms them from mysterious onslaughts into predictable events that can be prepared for and addressed systematically.

Common triggers for women include: conflict or the anticipation of conflict; situations requiring self-promotion or visibility; perceived criticism or disapproval; relationship uncertainty; transitions and change; physical symptoms that are interpreted as threatening; and the premenstrual hormonal shifts described in Chapter 2. Less commonly recognized triggers include: completing tasks successfully (which can trigger imposter syndrome anxiety about the next challenge); receiving praise (which can trigger the fear of being found out); and rest (which can trigger the anxiety of what is not being accomplished).

The practice of trigger identification is not about avoiding triggers — avoidance, as established earlier in this chapter, maintains anxiety. It is about having accurate information about when anxiety is most likely and being prepared with the appropriate tools. If you know that Sunday evenings reliably trigger anxiety about the week ahead, you can build a Sunday evening practice that addresses the anxiety proactively rather than being ambushed by it.

The Difference Between Anxiety and Intuition

One of the most practical questions anxious women ask is: how do I know the difference between anxiety telling me something is wrong and genuine intuition telling me something is wrong? This is a real question because anxious hypervigilance can look like intuition from the inside — both involve a sense of something being off that arrives before conscious reasoning.

The distinctions that are most reliable: genuine intuition tends to feel calm and certain, while anxiety tends to feel urgent and diffuse. Intuition is typically specific — this particular situation, this particular person — while anxiety generalizes. Intuition does not typically generate the rumination cycle that anxiety does; it arrives, registers, and settles. And genuine intuitive concern tends to be confirmed by subsequent events at a rate higher than chance, while anxious predictions tend to be disconfirmed more often than they are confirmed.

In practice, the most useful approach is to note the concern, not act on it immediately, and observe over time whether it is confirmed or disconfirmed. This is the opposite of what anxiety demands — which is immediate action to resolve the uncertainty. The capacity to hold uncertainty long enough to gather more information is itself a skill developed through the practices in this book.

Exercise: Your Avoidance Inventory

List every situation, conversation, or activity you have avoided in the past month because of anxiety. Be honest — include small avoidances as well as large ones. For each item, estimate: (1) How much relief did the avoidance provide? (2) What did the avoidance cost you? (3) What would you have done if anxiety were not a factor? The gap between what you do and what you would do without anxiety is the scope of the work this book addresses.

Key Takeaways

- Anxiety is a threat-detection system that evolved for physical dangers and over-activates in response to social, relational, and future-oriented concerns.
- Women's amygdalae are more reactive than men's on average, and estrogen amplifies this reactivity — making hormonal fluctuations a direct driver of anxiety.
- Anxiety maintains itself through avoidance, safety behaviors, and rumination — patterns that reduce anxiety short-term but amplify it long-term.
- The physical symptoms of anxiety are real but not dangerous — understanding them as anxiety rather than illness reduces the secondary anxiety that amplifies them.
- The path forward is systematic approach to anxiety-triggering situations, supported by the cognitive and somatic tools in this book.

CHAPTER 2

Hormonal Anxiety: Your Body Is Not the Enemy

If you have ever noticed that your anxiety feels significantly worse at certain points in the month, or that your tolerance for stress drops sharply before your period, or that the postpartum period brought a level of anxiety you had never experienced before — you are not imagining it. You are observing a real biological phenomenon that most anxiety resources never explain.

Hormones and anxiety are deeply intertwined. Understanding this relationship does not eliminate anxiety, but it does something almost as valuable: it removes the self-blame. When you understand that the anxiety spike you experience premenstrually is partly a hormonal event — not a sign that something is fundamentally wrong with you or that your life is falling apart — it becomes more manageable.

Estrogen, Progesterone, and the Anxious Brain

Estrogen has a complex relationship with anxiety. At optimal levels, estrogen has an anxiolytic effect — it supports the production of serotonin and reduces amygdala reactivity. This is why many women feel calmer, more emotionally resilient, and more socially confident during the follicular phase of the menstrual cycle, when estrogen is rising.

But when estrogen drops — as it does sharply in the premenstrual phase, and more gradually through perimenopause — that anxiolytic effect disappears, and the amygdala becomes more reactive. For women with premenstrual dysphoric disorder or significant premenstrual syndrome, this hormonal withdrawal can trigger anxiety that is clinically indistinguishable from a generalized anxiety episode.

Progesterone is metabolized in the brain into a compound called allopregnanolone, which acts on the same receptors as benzodiazepines — the class of medications most commonly prescribed for anxiety. When progesterone is at its peak in the luteal phase, allopregnanolone has a calming effect. But in women who are sensitive to hormonal changes, the same hormonal shifts that should be calming can paradoxically trigger anxiety — a phenomenon researchers are still working to fully understand.

Cortisol — the primary stress hormone — also interacts with estrogen in ways that are relevant to anxiety. Estrogen sensitizes the HPA axis, the system that regulates cortisol production. This means that women's cortisol response to stress is generally more robust than men's, producing higher and more prolonged cortisol elevations in response to the same stressors. Chronically elevated cortisol is itself anxiety-generating, creating a physiological feedback loop that makes anxiety self-perpetuating.

The Menstrual Cycle and Anxiety Mapping

One of the most practically useful things a woman with anxiety can do is track her anxiety in relation to her menstrual cycle. Most women who do this for two to three months begin to see a clear pattern: anxiety that felt random and overwhelming becomes predictable.

The typical pattern: relative calm and confidence in the follicular phase (days 1–14 for most women, counting from the first day of the period), a peak of well-being around ovulation, and then a gradual increase in anxiety, irritability, and emotional sensitivity through the luteal phase (days 15–28), peaking sharply in the premenstrual days before the period begins.

Knowing this pattern does not eliminate premenstrual anxiety. But it changes your relationship to it. Instead of "Why am I falling apart?" you can think "This is a predictable hormonal event, it will pass in a few days, and it does not reflect the actual state of my life or relationships." That reframe alone reduces the secondary anxiety — the anxiety about the anxiety — that often amplifies the original experience.

Tracking also allows for proactive management. If you know that your anxiety is reliably higher in the week before your period, you can schedule difficult conversations, high-stakes professional events, and other anxiety-amplifying situations at other points in the cycle when your resilience is higher. This is not avoidance — the situations are not being permanently avoided. It is strategic timing that works with your biology rather than against it.

Managing Anxiety Across the Cycle

The interventions most effective for hormonal anxiety address both the hormonal dimension and the anxiety that sits on top of it. On the hormonal side, the approaches with the strongest evidence include: regular aerobic exercise, which supports estrogen metabolism and reduces premenstrual mood symptoms; adequate magnesium and B6, which are involved in progesterone metabolism and GABA production; and reduction of caffeine and alcohol, which amplify hormonal mood symptoms.

For women with severe premenstrual anxiety — particularly those with a diagnosis of premenstrual dysphoric disorder — medical interventions including low-dose SSRIs (used specifically in the luteal phase rather than continuously) and hormonal treatments may be appropriate. These are conversations to have with a gynecologist or psychiatrist who specializes in women's mental health.

Postpartum Anxiety

The postpartum period involves the most dramatic hormonal shift of a woman's life: within 24 hours of delivery, progesterone and estrogen drop by roughly 100-fold. For most women, this hormonal withdrawal is accompanied by some degree of mood disturbance — the baby blues that affect up to 80% of new mothers in the first two weeks. For 15–20% of new mothers, the disturbance is more significant: postpartum anxiety, which can be as disabling as postpartum depression and is significantly underdiagnosed.

Postpartum anxiety often presents differently from depression. Rather than sadness and low energy, it appears as racing thoughts, inability to sleep even when the baby is sleeping, excessive worry about the baby's safety, hypervigilance, and a persistent sense of dread. It is treatable — with therapy, with medication if needed, and with the support structures addressed in Chapter 8.

If you are currently in the postpartum period and experiencing significant anxiety, please seek professional support without delay. Postpartum anxiety is not a sign of inadequate mothering. It is a medical condition with a biological basis and effective treatments. The sooner it is addressed, the faster recovery occurs — and recovery benefits not just the mother but the baby, whose developing regulatory system is directly influenced by the anxiety or calm of their primary caregiver.

Perimenopause and Anxiety

Perimenopause — the years of hormonal fluctuation before menopause, typically beginning in the mid-to-late forties — is one of the most underrecognized drivers of anxiety in midlife women. As estrogen levels become erratic and decline overall, the anxiolytic effect of estrogen is lost, and many women experience anxiety for the first time or find that previously manageable anxiety becomes significantly worse.

The anxiety of perimenopause is often accompanied by sleep disruption from night sweats, which compounds the problem: sleep deprivation is one of the most reliable anxiety amplifiers known. It can also present alongside cognitive symptoms — brain fog, word-finding difficulties — that create their own anxiety about cognitive decline.

Women in perimenopause often have their anxiety attributed to life circumstances — the challenges of midlife, empty nest, aging parents, career transitions — rather than to the hormonal changes that are genuinely driving or amplifying the experience. While life circumstances matter, the hormonal dimension deserves equal attention. Hormone therapy, where medically appropriate, can be transformative for perimenopausal anxiety. This is a conversation to have with a healthcare provider who is knowledgeable about perimenopause and its mental health implications.

The Thyroid Connection

The thyroid gland — which regulates metabolism, energy, and many other physiological processes — has a significant relationship with anxiety that is underappreciated in general anxiety literature. Both hyperthyroidism (overactive thyroid) and hypothyroidism (underactive thyroid) can produce anxiety symptoms. Hyperthyroidism produces anxiety, agitation, and panic that can be clinically indistinguishable from a primary anxiety disorder. Hypothyroidism, paradoxically, can also produce anxiety alongside fatigue and depression.

Women are significantly more likely than men to have thyroid conditions — estimates suggest that thyroid disorders affect women at approximately five to eight times the rate of men. If you have anxiety that has not responded to psychological treatment, or that is accompanied by changes in energy, weight, temperature regulation, or heart rate, thyroid function testing is worth discussing with your physician.

Exercise: Hormonal Anxiety Tracker

For the next two menstrual cycles, track your anxiety daily on a scale of 1–10 alongside the day of your cycle. Note also: sleep quality, major life stressors, and any significant anxiety events. After two cycles, look for patterns. Does anxiety reliably spike at the same phase? Is your premenstrual window predictable? This data is the foundation for managing hormonal anxiety more proactively – and for having an informed conversation with your healthcare provider if medical intervention is appropriate.

The Impact of Chronic Stress on Hormonal Anxiety

Chronic stress and hormonal anxiety interact in a feedback loop that deserves specific attention. The HPA axis is directly regulated by the same hormonal systems that produce the hormonal anxiety fluctuations described in this chapter. When chronic stress keeps cortisol elevated over time, it disrupts the normal hormonal cycle – affecting estrogen, progesterone, and the hypothalamic regulation of the entire reproductive hormonal system.

The practical implication is that chronic life stress amplifies hormonal anxiety beyond what the hormonal fluctuation alone would produce. The premenstrual week that is difficult under normal circumstances becomes significantly more difficult when chronic stress is also present. The perimenopausal anxiety that would be manageable in a supported, low-stress life becomes overwhelming when it coincides with significant life demands.

This is why the four pillars of Chapter 10 — sleep, movement, nutrition, and social connection — are particularly important for hormonally driven anxiety. They address the chronic stress load that amplifies hormonal effects. Reducing chronic stress does not eliminate hormonal anxiety, but it reduces the amplifier, making the hormonal fluctuations less overwhelming and the available coping capacity greater.

Communicating About Hormonal Anxiety

Hormonal anxiety is often invisible to others — including partners, employers, and family members — because it is intermittent rather than constant, and because the connection between hormonal phase and emotional state is not widely understood. This invisibility can be isolating and can lead to the anxiety being attributed to personality or relationship problems rather than its actual hormonal cause.

Educating the people in your life about hormonal anxiety — when you are in a calm phase, not during a high-anxiety period — can significantly reduce the relational consequences.

A partner who understands that the premenstrual week is a time of higher anxiety and lower stress tolerance can respond differently than one who interprets the same behavior as relationship dissatisfaction or personality instability. An employer who knows that you need to manage your schedule around a predictable high-stress window can be a resource rather than an obstacle.

The language that tends to be most effective is specific and biological: "I've noticed that my anxiety is reliably higher in the week before my period because of hormone changes. I'm working on managing it, and it helps if you know that if I seem more stressed than usual during that time, it's usually the hormones rather than anything specific to our relationship." This kind of clear, factual communication removes shame and creates the possibility of genuine support.

Exercise: Hormonal Anxiety Management Plan

Based on your cycle tracking, identify your two highest-anxiety days of the month. For those days, create a specific support plan: (1) Which somatic tools from Chapter 7 will you use? (2) What stressors or demands can be minimized on those days? (3) Who in your support network can you reach out to? (4) What self-care practices will you prioritize? Having a plan before the high-anxiety days arrive is significantly more effective than trying to improvise when you are in them.

Key Takeaways

- Hormonal fluctuations directly drive anxiety — estrogen withdrawal in the premenstrual phase, postpartum period, and perimenopause all reduce the brain's natural anxiety-buffering capacity.
- Tracking anxiety in relation to the menstrual cycle transforms what feels random into a predictable pattern, reducing the secondary anxiety about anxiety.
- Postpartum anxiety affects 15–20% of new mothers and is significantly underdiagnosed — it presents as racing thoughts, hypervigilance, and dread rather than sadness.
- Perimenopause is one of the most underrecognized drivers of new or worsening anxiety in midlife women — hormonal changes deserve attention alongside life circumstances.
- Thyroid conditions, which affect women at five to eight times the rate of men, can produce anxiety symptoms — thyroid function testing is worth considering for treatment-resistant anxiety.

CHAPTER 3

The People-Pleasing Trap and the Anxiety It Creates

People-pleasing is not a character trait. It is an anxiety management strategy — and a remarkably effective one in the short term. When you prioritize the happiness and approval of others, you reduce the immediate risk of conflict, disapproval, and rejection. The relief is real. The cost is enormous.

People-pleasing is one of the most significant drivers of anxiety in women, and one of the least recognized as such. Because it looks, from the outside, like generosity, kindness, and conscientiousness, it is rarely identified as a problem until the accumulation of unmet needs, chronic resentment, and exhaustion from constant self-monitoring becomes impossible to ignore.

The Origins of People-Pleasing

People-pleasing in women has both evolutionary and socialized roots. From an evolutionary perspective, the social bonds of female networks were survival-critical — women who maintained harmonious relationships were safer, had better access to resources, and were more effective caregivers. The sensitivity to social cues and the motivation to preserve relationships that drive people-pleasing behavior were adaptive.

From a socialized perspective, girls are systematically rewarded for being agreeable, accommodating, and relationally attuned, and penalized for being assertive, boundary-setting, or direct about their own needs. By adulthood, many women have internalized the belief — often unconscious — that their worth is contingent on their usefulness to others, and that expressing their own needs risks the disapproval and abandonment they fear.

In attachment terms, people-pleasing is a form of anxious attachment behavior: an attempt to maintain connection and security by anticipating and meeting others' needs, at the expense of one's own. Chapter 4 addresses attachment patterns and anxiety in depth.

The Anxiety-People-Pleasing Cycle

The relationship between people-pleasing and anxiety is bidirectional. Anxiety drives people-pleasing: when you are anxious about others' approval, you monitor their responses constantly, adjust your behavior to prevent disapproval, and say yes to requests even when your own needs conflict with compliance. And people-pleasing drives anxiety: the chronic suppression of your own needs creates a low-grade internal conflict that is itself anxiety-generating, and the performance demands of maintaining the people-pleasing role are exhausting in ways that deplete the nervous system's regulatory capacity.

There is also the specific anxiety of anticipating the consequences of stopping. For many people-pleasers, the prospect of setting a limit or declining a request generates acute anxiety — a fear of conflict, of the other person's hurt or anger, of the relationship being damaged beyond repair. This anxiety maintains the people-pleasing even when the person consciously wants to change.

The Internal Cost of People-Pleasing

The internal cost of chronic people-pleasing is rarely visible from the outside, which is part of why it is so difficult to address. The costs include: the resentment that builds when your own needs are consistently unmet; the exhaustion of constant self-monitoring and performance; the loss of authentic self-knowledge that occurs when you have been orienting toward others' preferences rather than your own for long enough; and the grief of realizing how much of your own life has been lived in service of others' comfort.

Chronic people-pleasers often have difficulty answering the question "What do you want?" Not because they are indecisive, but because the practice of suppressing and redirecting their own preferences has made those preferences genuinely harder to access. The recovery from people-pleasing is in part a process of rediscovering what you actually want, value, and need — a process that can feel strange and unfamiliar before it feels liberating.

Recognizing People-Pleasing in Your Own Life

People-pleasing exists on a spectrum. At one end are the relatively benign patterns most of us engage in sometimes: softening a difficult message, accommodating a preference we do not share, deferring to others in low-stakes decisions. At the other end are patterns that significantly compromise well-being: consistently prioritizing others' needs over your own, being unable to say no even when compliance is harmful, changing your position or suppressing your opinions based on others' reactions, and taking responsibility for managing others' emotions.

The question to ask is not whether you sometimes accommodate others — that is a sign of normal social intelligence. The question is whether the accommodation is chosen or compelled. Do you say yes because you want to, or because the anxiety of saying no is more than you can tolerate? Do you suppress your opinion because you genuinely do not have a strong view, or because you are monitoring the room for the "right" answer to give? The experience of compulsion — of having to rather than wanting to — is the marker of people-pleasing as an anxiety-driven pattern.

The Fear of Conflict and How to Work with It

Many people-pleasers identify conflict avoidance as the core driver of their pattern: the anxiety generated by the prospect of conflict or disapproval is so acute that avoiding it takes priority over almost everything else, including their own needs and well-being. Understanding this as an anxiety response — rather than a preference for harmony or a character trait of peacefulness — is crucial for changing it.

The anxiety of potential conflict has a characteristic cognitive signature: catastrophic predictions about what will happen if you say no or assert yourself. These predictions typically involve the other person's extreme negative reaction (rage, hurt, rejection) and the permanent damage to the relationship. Examining these predictions with the cognitive tools of Chapter 6 often reveals that they are significantly more catastrophic than the evidence supports.

What does actually happen when you are more assertive? In most relationships, the predicted catastrophe does not materialize. The other person is disappointed or frustrated, the conversation is uncomfortable, and then it passes. The relationship is not destroyed. Your needs are acknowledged. And you have updated your brain's threat assessment of assertiveness — slightly reducing its anxiety-generating power for next time.

Breaking the People-Pleasing Pattern

The antidote to people-pleasing is not becoming self-centered or indifferent to others. It is developing the capacity to tolerate the discomfort of disapproval without it driving your behavior. This is fundamentally an anxiety intervention: building the distress tolerance that allows you to hold your position, decline a request, or express a genuine opinion even when doing so generates the anxiety of potential conflict or rejection.

The techniques most effective for this are drawn from Acceptance and Commitment Therapy — specifically the practices of defusion (separating from the anxious thought rather than being controlled by it) and values-based action (acting from your values rather than from the drive to avoid discomfort). These techniques are introduced in Chapter 6.

Practically, breaking the people-pleasing pattern also involves developing new communication skills: learning to decline requests clearly and kindly without excessive justification; learning to express your own needs and preferences directly rather than hoping others will intuit them; and learning to tolerate the discomfort of others' disappointment without immediately moving to repair it at your own expense.

Exercise: Your People-Pleasing Audit

Spend 10 minutes listing the situations in your life where you most consistently prioritize others' needs over your own. For each situation, ask: (1) What am I afraid would happen if I said no or expressed my actual need? (2) Has that feared outcome actually happened when I have been more assertive in the past? (3) What does maintaining this pattern cost me? This audit builds the self-awareness that is the starting point for change.

The Physical Experience of Boundary-Setting

One of the most underappreciated aspects of boundary-setting for people-pleasers is its physical component. For women who have spent years or decades accommodating others, the experience of setting a limit often produces a characteristic physical anxiety response: heart pounding, stomach tightening, shallow breathing, a feeling of impending catastrophe. This response is not evidence that the limit-setting is wrong. It is evidence that the nervous system has learned to treat assertiveness as dangerous.

Understanding this physical response as a conditioned alarm rather than a genuine warning is essential for working through it. The somatic tools of Chapter 7 — particularly slow exhale breathing and grounding — applied immediately before and during boundary-setting reduce the physiological activation sufficiently to allow the limit to be held despite the anxiety. Over time, with repeated practice, the physical response diminishes as the nervous system learns through experience that assertiveness does not produce the predicted catastrophe.

People-Pleasing in Different Relationships

People-pleasing manifests differently in different types of relationships, and the barriers to changing it differ accordingly. In romantic partnerships, people-pleasing is often entangled with attachment anxiety — the fear that expressing your own needs will result in the partner's withdrawal or rejection. In friendships, it tends to be driven by the fear of conflict and the belief that the friendship can only be maintained through accommodation. In professional relationships, it is driven by power dynamics and the legitimate concern about the consequences of noncompliance.

Starting with the relationships where the consequences of assertiveness are most manageable is a sound strategy. Practicing assertiveness with friends or siblings before practicing it with a partner or a supervisor allows for the development of the skill and the updating of the anxious prediction in lower-stakes contexts. The experience of being more direct with a friend and discovering that the friendship survives and even deepens provides evidence that is transferable to higher-stakes relationships.

It is also worth acknowledging that some relationships are maintained primarily by people-pleasing — that the relationship exists because one person consistently accommodates the other, and that genuine reciprocity has not been established. When people-pleasing decreases in these relationships, the relationship may genuinely change — the other person may express dissatisfaction, may withdraw, or the relationship may end. This is painful but important information about the relationship's actual foundation.

Exercise: The Small No

This week, practice saying no to one low-stakes request where your instinct is to say yes out of anxiety rather than genuine desire. It does not need to be a significant request — the point is to practice the experience of declining and observing that the feared catastrophe does not materialize. Before declining, note your anxiety level (1–10). After declining and seeing the response, note it again. Repeat this weekly, gradually increasing the stakes of the requests you decline.

Key Takeaways

- People-pleasing is an anxiety management strategy, not a character trait — it reduces the immediate fear of disapproval at the cost of chronic need suppression and resentment.
- The relationship between people-pleasing and anxiety is bidirectional: anxiety drives people-pleasing and people-pleasing maintains anxiety.
- Chronic people-pleasing creates internal costs including resentment, exhaustion, and the gradual loss of access to your own authentic preferences and needs.
- The marker of problematic people-pleasing is the experience of compulsion — of having to rather than wanting to accommodate others.
- The antidote is the capacity to tolerate potential disapproval — a skill built through gradual, supported practice of more assertive behavior.

CHAPTER 4

Relationship Anxiety and Attachment Patterns

Relationships are simultaneously the greatest source of meaning in most people's lives and one of the most reliable sources of anxiety. For women with anxious attachment patterns, relationships are experienced not just as sources of connection and joy but as chronic sources of uncertainty, threat, and emotional labor.

Understanding your attachment style — the pattern of relating to others that was shaped in your earliest relationships — is one of the most practically useful things you can do for your anxiety. Not because knowing the pattern is sufficient to change it, but because the pattern is so automatic, so woven into how you perceive and respond to relational signals, that it is almost impossible to address without first making it visible.

Attachment Theory and Adult Anxiety

Attachment theory, originally developed by John Bowlby and subsequently expanded by researchers including Mary Ainsworth and Mary Main, describes the patterns of relating that develop from early experiences with caregivers. When early caregivers are consistently responsive and available, children develop secure attachment: a confident expectation that relationships are safe, that others can be relied upon, and that their own needs are legitimate and worthy of being met.

When early caregivers are inconsistently available — sometimes responsive, sometimes not, sometimes warm, sometimes cold or dismissive — children develop anxious or ambivalent attachment: a heightened alertness to relational cues, a chronic uncertainty about whether the attachment figure will be available when needed, and an amplified emotional response to perceived threats to the relationship.

Anxious attachment in adults looks like: preoccupation with partners or close friends, sensitivity to signs of distance or disapproval, a tendency to seek reassurance that can become exhausting for both parties, difficulty tolerating uncertainty in relationships, and a pattern of either amplifying emotional expression to get needs met or suppressing expression out of fear of being too much.

The Anxious Attachment Thought Patterns

Anxious attachment generates a characteristic set of thought patterns that are immediately recognizable to those who experience them. "Why hasn't she responded to my message? Is she angry with me?" "He seemed distracted tonight — am I doing something wrong?" "They liked everyone else's post but not mine." These thoughts share a common structure: an ambiguous relational signal is interpreted through the lens of potential abandonment or rejection, generating anxiety that drives the monitoring and reassurance-seeking behaviors that characterize anxious attachment.

The interpretive bias of anxious attachment is both the cause and the consequence of relationship anxiety. Anxious attachment inclines you to interpret neutral or ambiguous signals as negative — a delay in responding to a message becomes evidence of anger, a quiet evening becomes evidence of withdrawal. And this interpretive bias generates the anxiety that produces the behaviors (reassurance-seeking, clinging, pushing away) that genuinely do create relational distance, which then confirms the anxious interpretation.

Relationship Anxiety in Practice

Relationship anxiety is not confined to romantic partnerships. It appears in friendships, in family relationships, in professional relationships. The core fear is the same across contexts: that you are fundamentally not enough, that others will eventually discover this and withdraw, and that your survival of the relationship requires constant management of the other person's perceptions and responses.

The specific thoughts of relationship anxiety have a characteristic flavor: "Did I say something wrong?" "Are they pulling away?" "I am too much — I ask for too much, feel too much, need too much." These thoughts trigger the monitoring, reassurance-seeking, and accommodation behaviors that characterize anxious attachment, which maintain the underlying anxiety by preventing the development of genuine security.

Reassurance-seeking is the behavior that most clearly illustrates the short-term/long-term paradox of anxious attachment responses. Seeking reassurance from a partner that they still love you, that they are not angry, that the relationship is secure, produces immediate relief. But over time, repeated reassurance-seeking can genuinely create the relational distance it was seeking to prevent — because it communicates distrust and places a chronic emotional demand on the partner. And relief from reassurance is always temporary: the anxiety returns, often stronger, because the underlying threat assessment has not been updated.

Moving Toward Secure Functioning

The most hopeful finding from contemporary attachment research is that attachment patterns are not fixed. The attachment system is plastic — it can be updated through experiences of genuine security, whether with a consistently attuned partner, a skilled therapist, or through the practice of what some researchers call *earned security*: the deliberate cultivation of secure-functioning relationships that over time update the attachment system's expectations.

The practices most helpful for moving toward security in relationships include: learning to self-regulate emotionally rather than relying on the partner's response to manage your emotional state; developing the capacity to tolerate relational uncertainty without immediately acting to resolve it; and building the reflective function — the ability to understand your own and others' behavior in terms of underlying mental states — that is the cognitive foundation of secure attachment.

Therapy — particularly approaches that address the attachment system directly, such as Emotionally Focused Therapy for couples or attachment-informed individual therapy — can be transformative for anxious attachment. The therapeutic relationship itself provides a secure base: a consistently attuned, predictably available relationship that provides an experience of security that gradually updates the attachment system's expectations.

When Relationship Anxiety Is About the Relationship

An important caveat: not all relationship anxiety is anxious attachment. Sometimes the anxiety is a realistic response to a relationship that genuinely is uncertain, inconsistent, or unsafe. Distinguishing between anxiety that belongs to your attachment pattern and anxiety that is a realistic response to the relationship you are actually in requires honest self-examination — and sometimes requires the perspective of a therapist, trusted friend, or partner who can offer an outside view.

If your anxiety is highest in relationships where the other person is genuinely inconsistent, unreliable, or dismissive — and lower in relationships where others are genuinely warm and responsive — that is important information. The anxiety may be pointing to something real about the relationship rather than being entirely a function of your attachment pattern.

Exercise: Your Attachment Pattern

Reflect on your closest adult relationships and answer: (1) When you perceive distance or unavailability from someone important to you, what do you typically do — withdraw, seek reassurance, become upset, or something else? (2) How much mental space do your close relationships occupy — do you find yourself frequently thinking about how others feel about you? (3) Do you find it easy or difficult to ask for what you need directly? (4) When someone is kind and consistently available to you, do you trust it, or do you wait for something to go wrong? Your answers will illuminate your attachment pattern and where the work is.

Healing Anxious Attachment: The Long Game

Healing anxious attachment is a long-term project, not a quick fix. The attachment system was built through thousands of interactions over years of early experience, and it updates through thousands of new interactions over subsequent years. This is not discouraging — it means that every experience of genuine security, every instance of tolerating relational uncertainty without catastrophe, every moment of being honest about your needs and having them received with care, is contributing to the update.

The practices that most reliably contribute to earned security include: choosing relationships where consistency and responsiveness are genuinely present; learning to self-soothe rather than relying exclusively on others' reassurance; developing the reflective capacity to understand your own relational patterns as patterns rather than as reality; and — for those with the most significant attachment wounds — working with a skilled therapist who can provide the consistent, attuned relationship that is itself the healing experience.

Progress in healing anxious attachment is rarely linear. Stressful periods, hormonal shifts, and new relationship challenges often bring old patterns back to the surface. This does not represent a return to the starting point. It represents the way healing actually works — in spirals rather than straight lines, revisiting familiar territory at progressively greater levels of capacity to handle it.

The Role of Vulnerability in Reducing Relationship Anxiety

Paradoxically, one of the most effective ways to reduce relationship anxiety is to increase vulnerability — to share your genuine experience, including your anxiety, with the people you are closest to. This feels counterintuitive because anxiety typically tells you that vulnerability will confirm others' discovery of your inadequacy and precipitate the rejection you fear.

But genuine vulnerability — sharing your experience honestly, asking for what you need directly, allowing others to see you struggling — typically produces the opposite response in people who are genuine candidates for close relationship. It invites reciprocal vulnerability. It builds trust. It allows others to offer genuine support rather than responding only to the managed presentation. And it provides the experience of being known and accepted despite imperfection that is the foundation of genuine relational security.

The distinction between appropriate vulnerability and oversharing matters here. Appropriate vulnerability is sharing genuinely from a place of trusting relationship, seeking connection rather than reassurance or validation. Oversharing — which often accompanies anxious attachment — is flooding another person with anxiety content in a way that seeks reassurance, often before the relationship has the trust to hold it. The skill is calibrating vulnerability to the actual trust level of the relationship.

Exercise: Tolerating Relational Uncertainty

Choose one situation this week where you would normally seek reassurance — checking whether a partner is still happy, whether a friend is still interested, whether a colleague is pleased with your work. Instead of seeking reassurance, practice tolerating the uncertainty for 24 hours while noticing the anxiety without acting on it. What do you notice? Does the anxiety peak and then subside on its own? What information do you have at the end of 24 hours that you did not have at the start?

Key Takeaways

- Anxious attachment — a pattern of heightened alertness to relational threats and chronic uncertainty about others' availability — is one of the most common drivers of relationship anxiety.
- The interpretive bias of anxious attachment leads to reading neutral or ambiguous relational signals as negative, generating anxiety that produces behaviors that can create genuine distance.
- Reassurance-seeking provides temporary relief but maintains anxiety long-term by preventing the development of genuine relational security.
- Attachment patterns were shaped in early experience but are not fixed — they can be updated through consistent experiences of genuine relational security.
- Not all relationship anxiety is anxious attachment — sometimes it is a realistic response to a relationship that genuinely is inconsistent or unsafe.

CHAPTER 5

Imposter Syndrome and High-Achieving Women

Imposter syndrome — the persistent belief that you are not as competent as others perceive you to be, and that you will eventually be exposed as a fraud — was first identified by psychologists Pauline Clance and Suzanne Imes in 1978, in a study of high-achieving women. More than four decades of subsequent research has confirmed the pattern: it is significantly more common in women than men, and it is more common in women who are objectively high-achieving.

The paradox of imposter syndrome is that it does not diminish with success. For many women, each new achievement feels more like luck, more like convincing others of something that is not really true, more like one moment away from exposure. The very evidence that others point to as proof of competence — the promotion, the recognition, the successful project — is reinterpreted internally as proof of how well the deception is working.

The Anxiety Architecture of Imposter Syndrome

Imposter syndrome is not just a confidence issue. It is an anxiety pattern with a specific cognitive architecture. At its core is a fundamental disconnect between external evidence and internal belief: the external evidence says "you are competent," but the internal belief says "you are not, and they will find out." Anxiety is the experience of holding these two incompatible realities simultaneously and managing the constant threat that the external evidence will be shown to be false.

The behavioral consequences of imposter syndrome anxiety include: overworking to compensate for the supposed deficiency; difficulty accepting praise or attributing success to genuine competence; avoiding challenges that might "expose" the supposed lack; and an exhausting internal monitoring of whether others have yet noticed the fraud. These behaviors perpetuate the imposter experience by preventing the development of genuine competence confidence — the kind that comes from repeatedly doing things and finding that you can do them.

Why Women Are More Vulnerable

Imposter syndrome is more common in women for a combination of reasons that are social rather than biological. Women are more likely to have received competence-undermining messages in childhood and adolescence — direct or indirect messages that their intellectual or professional capabilities are less than those of their male peers. Women are more likely to be in environments where they are underrepresented, which makes the experience of not belonging more salient and persistent. And women are more likely to receive feedback that conflates performance with personal characteristics in ways that make failure feel more total.

The stereotype threat literature adds another dimension, though it should be cited carefully: early studies reported that women aware of negative stereotypes about their group's competence — women in STEM, women in finance, women in senior leadership — performed worse when the stereotype was made salient, but later replications with larger samples and corrections for publication bias have found the effect to be small at best. What is not in doubt is the experience itself: being aware that your competence may be judged against a stereotype about your group is a genuine and well-documented source of anxiety, and that anxiety feeds the imposter experience whatever its measured effect on performance.

The Perfectionism-Imposter Syndrome Connection

Perfectionism and imposter syndrome are closely linked in women. Perfectionism is the attempt to eliminate the gap between current performance and the standard that would prove genuine competence — but because the standard is set by the imposter belief rather than by realistic benchmarks, it is impossible to reach. Every achievement that meets the objective standard is reinterpreted by the imposter belief as a near-miss: "I got it done this time, but next time I might not."

The perfectionism driven by imposter syndrome is qualitatively different from healthy high standards. It is driven by fear rather than aspiration — by the need to prevent exposure rather than the desire to do excellent work. It produces overworking, paralysis in the face of good-enough, difficulty delegating or asking for help, and the exhaustion of standards that can never be definitively met.

Working with Imposter Syndrome

The most effective approaches to imposter syndrome combine cognitive and behavioral elements. On the cognitive side: learning to recognize imposter thoughts as thoughts rather than facts; building the practice of deliberately acknowledging evidence of competence; and developing a more differentiated sense of self that is not entirely contingent on professional performance.

On the behavioral side: deliberately approaching rather than avoiding challenges that feel exposing; learning to receive praise without immediately discounting it; and building relationships with mentors and peers in which authentic professional struggles can be discussed. The research on mentoring is particularly strong: women who have access to mentors who share their experiences of self-doubt are significantly less likely to interpret self-doubt as evidence of incompetence.

One of the most powerful interventions for imposter syndrome is normalizing: discovering through honest conversation with peers that the experience of self-doubt is not unique to you, that the colleagues you have been assuming are entirely confident are also experiencing uncertainty, and that feeling like an imposter does not mean you are one. The silence that surrounds professional self-doubt — particularly in competitive environments where admitting uncertainty feels dangerous — is itself one of the mechanisms that maintains imposter syndrome.

Exercise: The Evidence Audit

Take one area of your life where imposter syndrome is strongest. On one side of a page, list every piece of evidence that supports the imposter belief. On the other side, list every piece of evidence that contradicts it — credentials, outcomes, feedback, things you have learned and mastered. Notice what you do with the contradicting evidence: do you discount it, minimize it, explain it away? The discounting process is the imposter syndrome mechanism — seeing it clearly is the first step to interrupting it.

The Success Trap: When Achievement Increases Anxiety

One of the most disorienting experiences of imposter syndrome is the way it responds to success. Rather than diminishing with achievement, imposter syndrome anxiety often intensifies after success — because success raises the stakes. Each promotion, each accomplishment, each recognition expands the domain in which you could be exposed as inadequate. The more successful you are, the more you have to lose, and the more the imposter belief feels like a prediction that is always one slip away from being confirmed.

Understanding this dynamic is important because it prevents the mistaken conclusion that more achievement will eventually resolve the imposter experience. More achievement, without the cognitive and self-compassion work that addresses the underlying pattern, simply means more anxiety about more domains. The resolution of imposter syndrome comes not from achieving enough but from developing a relationship with your own competence that is grounded in evidence rather than in an unfalsifiable belief about fraudulence.

Imposter Syndrome in Mothers and Caregivers

Imposter syndrome extends beyond the professional domain in women — it appears with particular force in the domain of mothering and caregiving, where the stakes feel even higher and the feedback is less clear. The mother who feels that everyone else knows what they are doing, that she is making it up as she goes, that her children will eventually suffer the consequences of her inadequacy, is experiencing maternal imposter syndrome that is distinct from but related to professional imposter syndrome.

Maternal imposter syndrome is amplified by the same social factors that drive professional imposter syndrome: the idealization of motherhood as a natural and instinctive role that good mothers do effortlessly, the lack of honest conversation about the difficulty of parenting, and the comparison culture that social media has intensified — a constant stream of curated parenting successes that distorts the perception of what other mothers' actual experience is.

The same interventions that work for professional imposter syndrome apply here: making explicit the evidence of adequate caregiving; normalizing the struggle through honest conversations with other parents; developing defusion from thoughts like "I am not a good enough mother"; and building a more grounded, evidence-based assessment of what good enough parenting actually requires — which research consistently shows is significantly more achievable than the perfectionistic standard suggests.

Exercise: The Mentor Conversation

Identify one person in your professional life whose competence you respect and who you assume does not experience self-doubt. If you have a relationship that allows it, ask them directly: do you ever feel like you don't really know what you're doing, or that others will figure out you're not as capable as they think? Most people, when asked honestly, will share their version of the imposter experience. This conversation can be more valuable than any amount of self-analysis.

Separating Self-Worth from Professional Performance

One of the deepest drivers of imposter syndrome is the conflation of professional performance with personal worth. When your sense of who you are as a person is contingent on how well you perform at work, any professional difficulty becomes an existential threat rather than a practical problem. The amygdala responds to existential threats the same way it responds to physical threats — with the full anxiety response — which explains why imposter syndrome anxiety can feel so disproportionate to the actual professional stakes.

Building a sense of self that is not contingent on professional performance is not the same as becoming less committed to your work or less motivated to do it well. It is developing what psychologists call noncontingent self-esteem: a stable sense of worth that is not subject to the fluctuations of performance, feedback, and outcomes. Women with noncontingent self-esteem are not less professional — they are more resilient, more willing to take risks, and more capable of learning from failure because failure is not a threat to who they are.

The practice of building noncontingent self-esteem involves identifying the values and qualities that constitute who you are independent of your professional role: how you treat people, what you care about, the things that matter to you outside of work, the relationships you invest in. These dimensions of self are not subject to performance review and do not fluctuate with project outcomes. Building explicit awareness of them is a counter to the imposter syndrome mechanism that makes professional performance the totality of identity.

The Comparison Trap: When You Are Surrounded by Exceptional People

Imposter syndrome is significantly amplified by certain environments — specifically, high-achieving environments where you are surrounded by people who appear uniformly competent, confident, and capable. Graduate programs, top-tier companies, elite professional environments are filled with people who have been selected for capability. The result is a statistical guarantee of a specific distortion: when the people around you are all in the top percentile of performers, the average of the group you compare yourself to is far above the actual average. Your comparisons are inherently distorting.

The research on this phenomenon — called the big-fish-little-pond effect — shows that high-achieving individuals placed in high-achieving environments consistently rate their own ability lower than identically capable individuals placed in average environments. The environment sets the comparison standard, and in elite environments, the standard is set so high that genuine competence feels like inadequacy.

Correcting for this requires a deliberate recalibration of the comparison standard. Who are you comparing yourself to, and is that comparison accurate? Are you comparing your internal experience — which includes all your uncertainty and self-doubt — with others' external presentations — which conceals theirs? Are you comparing yourself to the most exceptional people in your environment rather than to a representative sample? Accurate comparison requires honest information, and honest information about others' experience of self-doubt is rarely available unless you ask for it directly.

Building Genuine Competence Confidence

Genuine competence confidence — as opposed to the performance of confidence that imposter syndrome demands — develops through a specific mechanism: doing difficult things, noticing that you can do them, and allowing that evidence to update your self-assessment. This sounds simple, but imposter syndrome disrupts the mechanism at the last step. The evidence accumulates — the difficult things get done — but the internal belief does not update because each success is attributed to external factors rather than to competence.

The intervention is to make the attribution process explicit. After a success, instead of automatically attributing it to luck or circumstances, deliberately ask: what role did my competence play in this outcome? What skills did I use? What did I know that contributed to the result? What decisions did I make well? This does not require overclaiming — it requires accurately crediting your contribution to outcomes that you tend to attribute entirely elsewhere.

Over time, this practice builds what researchers call a growth identity: a sense of yourself as someone who develops competence through effort and learning rather than someone who either has it or does not. A growth identity is significantly more robust to the imposter experience because it does not require you to already be completely competent — it frames your current state as the expected and acceptable starting point for continued development.

Exercise: The Weekly Accomplishment Log

For the next four weeks, spend five minutes at the end of each week writing down three things you did well. Not three things that went perfectly — three things to which you contributed genuine competence. Include the specific skill or knowledge that contributed to each outcome. After four weeks, read back through the log. Notice whether the picture that emerges matches your internal sense of yourself as a competent professional. The gap between the record and the internal sense is the imposter syndrome mechanism — seeing it clearly begins to close it.

Key Takeaways

- Imposter syndrome is an anxiety pattern, not a confidence problem — it involves a persistent disconnect between external evidence of competence and internal belief.
- Women are more vulnerable to imposter syndrome for social reasons — competence-undermining messages, underrepresentation, and stereotype threat — not biological ones.
- Perfectionism driven by imposter syndrome is fear-based rather than aspiration-based, producing overworking and impossible standards rather than genuine excellence.
- The most effective approaches combine cognitive restructuring of imposter thoughts, behavioral approach of avoided challenges, and the normalization that comes from honest conversations with peers.

CHAPTER 6

Rewiring the Anxious Brain: CBT and ACT for Women

The two most extensively researched psychological approaches to anxiety are Cognitive Behavioral Therapy and Acceptance and Commitment Therapy. Both have strong evidence bases. Both are effective for anxiety. And they complement each other in ways that make using them together more powerful than using either alone.

CBT works primarily by changing the content of anxious thinking — identifying distorted or unhelpful thoughts and replacing them with more accurate and balanced alternatives. ACT works by changing your relationship to anxious thoughts — developing the capacity to observe them without being controlled by them, and redirecting your behavior toward your values regardless of what your anxiety is saying.

CBT: Changing the Content of Anxious Thoughts

The foundational CBT model of anxiety is simple: our thoughts about situations drive our emotional responses, and those emotional responses drive our behavior. An event is not inherently anxiety-producing — our interpretation of it is. Changing the interpretation changes the emotional and behavioral response.

The most common anxious thought patterns — sometimes called *cognitive distortions* — include: catastrophizing (assuming the worst possible outcome is the most likely one), mind reading (assuming you know what others are thinking, usually negatively), fortune telling (treating negative future predictions as facts), all-or-nothing thinking (seeing situations in black and white with no middle ground), and personalization (taking excessive personal responsibility for outcomes that are not fully in your control).

The CBT technique for addressing these patterns is called cognitive restructuring: identifying the specific distorted thought, examining the evidence for and against it, and generating a more balanced alternative. This is not positive thinking — it is accurate thinking. The goal is not to convince yourself that everything will be fine, but to arrive at a realistic assessment that reflects all available evidence rather than just the anxiety-amplifying interpretation.

Cognitive Distortions Most Common in Women

While all the cognitive distortions affect both men and women, certain patterns appear with particular frequency in the female anxiety presentations described in this book. Personalization — taking excessive responsibility for others' emotional states — is the cognitive engine of both people-pleasing and maternal anxiety. Mind reading — assuming you know what others think, usually negatively — drives social anxiety and relationship anxiety. Catastrophizing — treating uncertain futures as certainly catastrophic — underlies health anxiety, maternal anxiety, and the anxiety of high-achievers who cannot afford to fail.

For women who have been socialized to be attuned to others, mind reading has a particular character: it is often not experienced as a cognitive distortion at all, but as accurate social perception. "I know she's upset with me" feels like reading the room correctly, not like a distorted interpretation of ambiguous cues. Learning to distinguish between genuine social reading and anxiety-driven mind reading — and to apply the same evidential scrutiny to social interpretations as to other anxious thoughts — is a specific skill that many women need to develop.

ACT: Changing Your Relationship to Anxious Thoughts

Where CBT targets the content of anxious thoughts, ACT targets the process — specifically, the process of fusion, in which you are so merged with your thoughts that you experience them as reality rather than as mental events.

Defusion is the core ACT technique for anxiety. Instead of engaging with the content of an anxious thought — arguing with it, trying to disprove it, or being controlled by it — defusion involves stepping back and observing the thought as a thought. The anxious thought "I am going to fail" becomes "I notice I am having the thought that I am going to fail." This seemingly small linguistic shift creates cognitive distance that reduces the thought's ability to drive behavior.

ACT also introduces the concept of values-based action: acting in accordance with your deepest values regardless of what your anxiety is telling you. This is the direct antidote to avoidance — instead of asking "What does my anxiety want me to do?" you ask "What would the person I want to be do in this situation?" This reorientation from anxiety-avoidance to values-approach is one of the most powerful behavioral shifts available to people working with anxiety.

The Observer Self

One of the most distinctive contributions of ACT to anxiety treatment is the concept of the observer self — the part of your awareness that can observe your thoughts, feelings, and experiences without being identical to them. When you are fused with anxiety, you are the anxiety: "I am an anxious person." When you contact the observer self, you can say: "I am having anxiety right now. I am the awareness that observes the anxiety, not the anxiety itself."

Developing the observer perspective is practiced through mindfulness — the intentional, nonjudgmental observation of present-moment experience. Mindfulness is not relaxation (though it may produce relaxation as a byproduct). It is the practice of noticing what is happening — including anxious thoughts and feelings — without immediately reacting to it. This creates the space between stimulus and response in which the choice to act from values rather than from anxiety becomes possible.

Applying CBT and ACT to Women's Specific Anxiety Patterns

For people-pleasing anxiety, the CBT intervention targets the catastrophic beliefs about what will happen if you set a limit or say no. What exactly do you believe will happen? How likely is that outcome, realistically? What has happened in the past when you have been more direct? The ACT intervention targets the avoidance driving the people-pleasing: instead of acting from the anxiety of potential disapproval, acting from the value of authentic relationship.

For imposter syndrome anxiety, the CBT intervention targets the discounting of competence evidence and the amplification of failure evidence. The ACT intervention targets the fusion with thoughts like "I am a fraud" — practicing defusion so these thoughts can be observed without being acted on through avoidance and overworking.

For relationship anxiety, the CBT intervention targets the mind-reading and catastrophic interpretations of relational uncertainty. The ACT intervention targets the reassurance-seeking behavior — accepting the uncertainty of not knowing exactly where you stand, while acting from the value of genuine connection rather than from the drive to eliminate relational uncertainty.

Exercise: Thought Record

For the next week, keep a simple thought record when you notice anxiety. Write: (1) The situation. (2) The anxious thought — exactly what did your mind say? (3) The cognitive distortion — which pattern does this match? (4) The evidence for and against the thought. (5) A more balanced alternative. (6) Rate your anxiety before and after the restructuring (0–10). After a week, review: do the same distortions appear repeatedly? Recognizing your most common patterns is more useful than trying to address every anxious thought individually.

Behavioral Experiments: Testing Anxious Predictions

One of the most powerful CBT techniques for anxiety is the behavioral experiment: a structured test of an anxious prediction that provides real-world evidence about whether the prediction is accurate. Unlike cognitive restructuring, which works with the content of anxious thoughts in the abstract, behavioral experiments work with reality — they put the prediction to a direct test and gather actual data.

The structure of a behavioral experiment: (1) Identify the anxious prediction clearly ("If I express a different opinion in this meeting, others will think I am incompetent and exclude me"); (2) Rate your confidence in the prediction from 0 to 100%; (3) Design a specific test ("I will express one clear opinion in the next meeting and observe what happens"); (4) Conduct the experiment; (5) Record what actually happened; (6) Compare the actual outcome to the prediction and revise your prediction accordingly.

Behavioral experiments are more powerful than cognitive restructuring alone because they generate first-hand evidence rather than theoretical counter-arguments. The brain is more responsive to direct experience than to logical argument. When you discover through experience that expressing an opinion did not result in exclusion, that evidence updates the threat assessment in a way that thinking about it never quite can.

Working with Chronic Worry

Generalized anxiety — the kind that does not attach specifically to social situations, or relationships, or professional performance, but floods across all domains — typically has chronic worry as its primary cognitive component. The worry feels productive — like problem-solving, like preparation — but it is not. Research consistently shows that worry does not improve outcomes, does not generate useful solutions, and does not provide the preparation it promises. It maintains anxiety and depletes the cognitive resources needed for genuine problem-solving.

The most effective CBT interventions for chronic worry include: worry postponement, in which worrying is deliberately limited to a scheduled 15-minute period rather than allowed to run throughout the day; the distinction between solvable and unsolvable worries, with problem-solving applied to the former and defusion applied to the latter; and the development of tolerance for uncertainty, which underlies most chronic worry.

Tolerance for uncertainty is the keystone capacity for chronic worry. Worry is fundamentally an attempt to resolve uncertainty through mental simulation — to figure out what might happen and prepare for it. But uncertainty about future events is irreducible, and the attempt to resolve it through worry simply perpetuates the anxious state. Developing the capacity to hold uncertainty — to know that you cannot predict or control all future outcomes and to continue functioning anyway — is more effective than any amount of worry.

Mindfulness and Anxiety

Mindfulness occupies an important place in contemporary anxiety treatment, particularly through its integration into Mindfulness-Based Cognitive Therapy and through its foundational role in ACT. The research on mindfulness and anxiety is strong: regular mindfulness practice reduces anxiety symptoms, reduces the tendency to ruminate, and increases the capacity for emotional regulation.

Mindfulness works for anxiety through several mechanisms. It interrupts the automatic nature of anxious thinking — creating a moment of awareness between the trigger and the response. It develops the observer perspective that is the foundation of defusion. It builds the capacity to hold difficult experiences without immediately acting to change them. And it trains the attentional system, which chronic anxiety has biased toward threat detection, to attend to a broader range of experience.

Formal mindfulness practice — sitting meditation, body scan, mindful movement — develops the capacity most reliably. But informal mindfulness — bringing full attention to everyday activities, noticing sensory experience, pausing between activities to observe the present moment — is accessible throughout the day and accumulates significant benefit over time. Beginning with five minutes of daily formal practice and expanding gradually is more effective than ambitious commitments that are difficult to sustain.

Exercise: Defusion Practice

Take one recurring anxious thought — one that shows up frequently and that you tend to be fused with. Write it as you normally experience it: "I am going to make a mistake and everyone will see how incompetent I am." Now rewrite it in defusion language: "I notice I am having the thought that I am going to make a mistake and everyone will see how incompetent I am." Say both versions aloud. Notice whether the defusion version creates any distance from the thought. Practice the defusion version three times a day for one week.

Key Takeaways

- CBT changes the content of anxious thoughts through cognitive restructuring; ACT changes your relationship to thoughts through defusion and values-based action.
- Cognitive distortions — catastrophizing, mind reading, fortune telling, all-or-nothing thinking, personalization — are the specific thought patterns that CBT targets.
- For women, mind reading has a particular character: it feels like accurate social perception rather than a cognitive distortion, requiring specific attention.
- Defusion — observing thoughts as mental events rather than being fused with them — is the core ACT technique for reducing anxiety's control over behavior.
- The observer self — the awareness that can notice anxiety without being identical to it — is developed through mindfulness practice.

CHAPTER 7

The Nervous System Reset: Somatic Tools That Work

Anxiety is not only a cognitive phenomenon. It is a full-body experience — a physiological state in which the nervous system is in a state of heightened activation, the muscles are braced, breathing is shallow, heart rate is elevated, and the body is mobilized for a threat that, in most cases, is not physical.

Cognitive tools — the CBT and ACT techniques of Chapter 6 — address anxiety through the mind. Somatic tools address anxiety through the body. Both are necessary. The reason cognitive tools alone are often insufficient is that when the nervous system is in a state of significant activation, the brain's capacity for the kind of reflective thought that cognitive restructuring requires is genuinely compromised. The prefrontal cortex — the part of the brain responsible for rational thought, perspective-taking, and executive function — is relatively suppressed under high activation. You cannot think your way out of a state in which thinking is impaired.

The Autonomic Nervous System

The autonomic nervous system regulates the body's basic functions — heart rate, breathing, digestion, immune response — and has two primary branches. The sympathetic branch drives the stress response: when activated, it elevates heart rate, speeds breathing, suppresses digestion, and floods the body with stress hormones. The parasympathetic branch drives the rest-and-digest response: when dominant, it slows heart rate, deepens breathing, and allows the body to repair and restore.

Anxiety is a state of sympathetic dominance. Somatic anxiety tools work by activating the parasympathetic system — specifically by stimulating the vagus nerve, the longest nerve in the body, which runs from the brainstem to the abdomen and is the primary pathway of parasympathetic regulation.

Polyvagal theory, proposed by researcher Stephen Porges, offers a widely used vocabulary for these states, though its neurophysiology is contested and its central anatomical premise has been challenged in the research literature. As a descriptive map rather than settled anatomy, it names three states: the ventral vagal state (safe and connected — the foundation of genuine calm and authentic social engagement), the sympathetic state (fight-or-flight — mobilization for threat), and the dorsal vagal state (freeze and shutdown — immobilization in the face of overwhelming threat). Treat this as a useful description of how the states feel rather than as established biology — the practices in this chapter are supported on their own evidence, independently of it. Noticing which state you are in is still the first step in choosing the intervention most likely to help.

Vagal Tone and Anxiety

Vagal tone refers to the activity of the vagus nerve and is a reliable predictor of anxiety vulnerability. People with higher vagal tone recover from stress more quickly, regulate their emotions more effectively, and are less reactive to threatening stimuli. The good news is that vagal tone is not fixed — it can be increased through specific practices.

Slow diaphragmatic breathing is the most well-researched vagal activation technique. Specifically, breathing with a longer exhale than inhale — such as inhaling for four counts and exhaling for six to eight counts — activates the parasympathetic branch more strongly than the sympathetic. This is because heart rate increases on the inhale (sympathetic) and decreases on the exhale (parasympathetic). A longer exhale extends the period of parasympathetic dominance.

Humming, singing, and gargling also activate the vagus nerve through vibration of the vocal cords, which are innervated by vagal branches. Cold water exposure — particularly splashing cold water on the face or immersing the face in cold water — triggers the diving reflex, which rapidly activates the parasympathetic system. These may sound like unusual anxiety interventions, but the research supporting them is solid.

Somatic Grounding Techniques

Grounding techniques work by bringing attention into the present body and physical environment, interrupting the forward-projecting quality of anxious thought. The 5-4-3-2-1 technique — naming five things you can see, four you can touch, three you can hear, two you can smell, one you can taste — is one of the most widely used because it can be done anywhere without being visible to others.

Progressive muscle relaxation — systematically tensing and releasing muscle groups throughout the body — works by introducing conscious relaxation where the body has been holding unconscious tension. Most people with chronic anxiety are not aware of how much muscular tension they are carrying until they deliberately release it. Even 10 minutes of progressive muscle relaxation produces measurable reductions in physiological anxiety markers.

Body scanning — moving attention systematically through the body from feet to head, noticing sensations without trying to change them — combines the attention-training benefits of mindfulness with the physiological effects of grounding. It is particularly useful for women who have developed a disconnected relationship with their bodies, which is common in those who have experienced chronic stress, difficult body-image experiences, or trauma.

Movement as Nervous System Regulation

Physical movement is one of the most effective anxiety interventions available, and one of the most underutilized. The stress hormones that anxiety produces — cortisol, adrenaline — were designed to be metabolized through physical activity. In the absence of physical movement, they linger in the system and maintain the anxious state.

The research on exercise and anxiety is consistent and strong. Aerobic exercise produces anxiolytic effects comparable to medication for mild to moderate anxiety, with effects that build over time with regular practice. But even a 10-minute walk is sufficient to produce measurable reductions in cortisol and anxiety symptoms. The goal is not athletic performance — it is nervous system regulation.

Yoga and other mind-body movement practices deserve particular mention for their evidence base in anxiety. Yoga combines the benefits of physical movement with controlled breathing, body awareness, and mindfulness — addressing multiple anxiety maintenance mechanisms simultaneously. The research on yoga and anxiety is particularly strong for women, and it has an additional benefit that is not shared by many other forms of exercise: it tends to improve the relationship with the body rather than instrumentalizing it.

The Role of Touch in Nervous System Regulation

Physical touch — from others and from oneself — is a powerful nervous system regulator through its effects on the oxytocin system. Oxytocin, sometimes called *the bonding hormone*, has direct anxiolytic effects and is released through gentle, warm touch. In the presence of a trusted other person, touch produces co-regulation — the mutual calming of two nervous systems through physical contact.

Self-touch — placing a hand on the heart, on the cheek, or on the belly — also activates the oxytocin system and can be practiced privately in anxious moments. This may sound simple to the point of being trivial, but the research on self-compassion touch is genuine: the physiological response to warm, gentle self-touch is measurable and meaningful.

Exercise: Build Your Somatic Toolkit

This week, practice one somatic technique daily for at least five minutes. Options: (1) Extended exhale breathing: inhale for four, exhale for seven, for five minutes. (2) Progressive muscle relaxation: tense and release each muscle group from feet to face. (3) Grounding walk: walk for 10 minutes noticing only physical sensations. (4) Yoga or gentle stretching with attention to breath. After a week, notice which technique produces the most relief for you. That is your primary tool — the one to reach for first when anxiety is high.

Creating a Daily Nervous System Regulation Practice

Managing anxiety is not only about responding to acute episodes. It is about daily maintenance of the nervous system's regulatory capacity — keeping the baseline activation low enough that acute triggers do not produce overwhelming responses. This requires building daily regulation practices into the structure of your life, not just reaching for them when anxiety is already high.

The most effective daily regulation practices take 5–20 minutes and fit into existing routine. Morning practices that include some form of regulated breathing, body awareness, or gentle movement establish a regulated baseline for the day. Evening practices that support the transition from sympathetic activation to the parasympathetic state needed for sleep — avoiding screens, using extended exhale breathing, progressive muscle relaxation — protect sleep quality and the next day's anxiety baseline.

Midday practices — even a five-minute grounding walk, a brief body scan, or three minutes of physiological sighs — interrupt the accumulation of stress activation that occurs through a typical workday. These brief interruptions prevent the cortisol buildup that makes late-afternoon and evening anxiety so common.

Anxiety First Aid: When Anxiety Spikes

Despite the best maintenance practices, anxiety will spike. Premenstrual hormonal shifts, sleep disruption, significant stressors, unexpected threats — all of these will produce acute anxiety regardless of how well-maintained the baseline is. Having a specific, pre-decided anxiety first aid protocol reduces the time spent in high activation because it removes the need to figure out what to do while in a state where decision-making is impaired.

A basic anxiety first aid sequence: first, physiological sigh (double inhale, long exhale) three times — this produces the fastest parasympathetic shift available; second, grounding (name five things you see) to interrupt the forward-projecting thought loop; third, self-compassion touch (hand on heart) with the self-compassion break ("This is hard. Many people feel this. May I be kind to myself."); fourth, extended exhale breathing for five minutes. This sequence addresses the physiological, cognitive, and emotional dimensions of acute anxiety in a systematic way.

The key to anxiety first aid working is having it decided before it is needed. When anxiety is high, the decision about what to do is itself anxiety-generating. Having a specific, practiced protocol that you implement automatically reduces this burden. Practice the sequence when you are calm so that the individual steps are familiar when you need them under pressure.

Exercise: The Physiological Sigh

One of the fastest vagal activation techniques is the physiological sigh: take a normal inhale, then add a second, shorter inhale on top of it (a double inhale), then release with a long, slow exhale. This technique reduces the carbon dioxide buildup that contributes to anxiety symptoms faster than single-breath techniques. Practice it three times right now. Then practice it whenever you notice the first signs of anxiety activation — before the anxiety builds momentum.

Key Takeaways

- Anxiety is a physiological state of sympathetic nervous system activation — cognitive tools alone are insufficient because high activation impairs the reflective thought they require.
- Vagal tone — the activity of the vagus nerve — is a reliable predictor of anxiety vulnerability and can be increased through specific practices including slow exhale breathing and cold exposure.
- Grounding techniques including 5-4-3-2-1, progressive muscle relaxation, and body scanning interrupt anxious rumination by bringing attention into the present body.
- Physical movement metabolizes stress hormones and produces anxiolytic effects comparable to medication for mild to moderate anxiety.
- Touch — from others and from oneself — activates the oxytocin system and produces direct anxiolytic effects through nervous system co-regulation.

CHAPTER 8

Maternal Anxiety and the Invisible Mental Load

Motherhood is the role that women's culture most idealizes and the one that creates the most anxiety in practice. The idealization is the problem: when motherhood is presented as the most natural, fulfilling, and instinctive of roles — one that a good mother does effortlessly and joyfully — the inevitable gap between that image and the actual experience of motherhood becomes not just disappointing but shaming.

Anxiety is one of the most common experiences of new and experienced mothers alike, and one of the least discussed. The stigma of maternal anxiety — the fear that admitting it means you are not a good mother, that you do not love your child enough, that something is fundamentally wrong with you — keeps it private and untreated far longer than it should be.

The Invisible Mental Load

The mental load of motherhood — the cognitive and emotional labor of tracking, planning, anticipating, and managing the needs of a family — falls disproportionately on women in most households, regardless of whether the woman works outside the home. This is not simply about task division. It is about the default assignment of cognitive and managerial responsibility: who knows when the pediatric appointment is, who tracks what is needed at school, who anticipates that the winter coats need to come out, who manages the emotional calendar of the family.

The mental load is anxiety-generating not just because of its volume but because of its nature: it consists of an unending series of potential failures. Every item on the mental load is a potential thing that could go wrong if not tracked correctly. This creates a chronic low-grade state of vigilance — the nervous system equivalent of keeping many browser tabs open simultaneously — that is physiologically exhausting and that makes genuine recovery from anxiety impossible.

The mental load is also invisible — invisible to partners who are not carrying it, invisible to the outside world, and often invisible even to the women carrying it until they are asked to make it explicit. Making the mental load visible is the first step toward addressing it — not just as a fairness issue within relationships, but as an anxiety issue that requires structural change to address.

Maternal Anxiety vs. Maternal Worry

There is an important distinction between maternal worry — the normal concern for a child's well-being that is universal in parents — and maternal anxiety, which is persistent, intrusive, and interferes with functioning. Most mothers worry. Maternal anxiety is something different: intrusive thoughts about harm coming to the child, compulsive checking behaviors, avoidance of situations perceived as dangerous, and a persistent sense of dread that does not respond to reassurance.

The intrusive thoughts of maternal anxiety deserve particular attention. It is extremely common for new parents to experience intrusive thoughts — unwanted mental images of harm coming to the baby, including harm that the parent themselves might cause. These thoughts are deeply disturbing and are almost never discussed because of the shame they generate. They are not, however, predictive of behavior. Research consistently shows that intrusive thoughts about harming a baby are more common in parents with strong attachment to the baby — the very people least likely to act on them. The thoughts are a feature of anxious hypervigilance, not a sign of danger.

The Perfectionism of Motherhood

Contemporary motherhood in many cultures has become characterized by an unprecedented level of intensive engagement — a standard of parental involvement, stimulation, and optimization of child development that is qualitatively different from what previous generations experienced or expected. This intensive parenting culture places extraordinary demands on mothers in particular, and creates a perfectionism that is guaranteed to generate anxiety.

The specific perfectionism of modern motherhood involves the belief that children's outcomes are largely determined by parental choices and behaviors — choices about feeding, education, stimulation, attachment, and a hundred other domains in which the "right" choice is contested, the evidence is mixed, and the emotional stakes are impossibly high. This perfectionism is anxiety-generating not because it reflects reality (child development research is consistently more optimistic about the range of adequate parenting than the perfectionism standard suggests) but because it creates an unending audit of choices against an impossible standard.

Reducing Maternal Anxiety

Reducing maternal anxiety requires addressing both the cognitive and the structural. The cognitive work — challenging catastrophic maternal thoughts, developing defusion from intrusive thoughts, building distress tolerance — uses the same CBT and ACT tools described in Chapter 6, applied to the specific content of maternal anxiety.

The structural work requires addressing the mental load directly. This means explicit conversations with partners about the cognitive labor of parenting, not just task division. It means building genuine support networks rather than relying on the nuclear family unit to meet all caregiving needs. It means challenging the intensive parenting standard not through indifference to children's well-being but through more accurate information about what children actually need and what range of parenting is genuinely adequate.

Self-compassion is the specific antidote to the shame-amplified anxiety of maternal anxiety. The shame that surrounds maternal anxiety — the sense that a good mother would not feel this way — amplifies the anxiety it accompanies, because shame is itself a threat state that activates the stress response. Treating yourself with the same compassion you would offer a friend who told you she was experiencing maternal anxiety is not just kind — it is clinically meaningful.

Exercise: Mental Load Audit

Map your current mental load. Write down every ongoing cognitive responsibility you carry — everything you track, plan, anticipate, and manage for your family. Be comprehensive. Then: (1) Identify which items are genuinely yours to carry and which are defaults that could be shared or delegated. (2) Estimate how many hours per week the mental load occupies your cognitive attention. (3) Consider what a realistic conversation about mental load redistribution would look like with your partner or support network.

Anxiety and the Postpartum Body

The relationship between the postpartum body and anxiety deserves specific attention because it is a dimension that most anxiety resources overlook. Physical recovery from childbirth — whether vaginal or cesarean — is significant, unpredictable, and in many cultural contexts insufficiently supported. The pain, fatigue, and physical vulnerability of the postpartum period create a physiological state that is itself anxiety-amplifying, independent of the hormonal changes.

Sleep deprivation in the newborn period is among the most reliably anxiety-amplifying experiences known. Even the most resilient nervous system, under conditions of severe sleep fragmentation, will show increased amygdala reactivity, reduced prefrontal regulation, elevated cortisol, and impaired emotional processing. This is not a sign of inadequacy. It is a normal physiological response to conditions that are genuinely stressful.

Body image concerns also intensify postpartum anxiety for many women. The postpartum body is different — in ways that are normal, expected, and the result of growing a human being — and cultural pressure to "bounce back" creates a specific anxiety about physical inadequacy on top of the other demands of new parenthood. Addressing this with the same self-compassion practices described in Chapter 12 is important: the postpartum body deserves the same warmth and acceptance as any other aspect of the self that is struggling.

Supporting Yourself Through Maternal Anxiety

Maternal anxiety exists in a cultural context that makes asking for help particularly difficult. The expectation that mothers should be able to manage with minimal support, and the stigma of admitting difficulty, keeps many mothers isolated with anxiety that is both common and treatable. Building the support structures that reduce isolation is one of the most important structural interventions for maternal anxiety.

Practical support structures include: connection with other parents who can normalize the struggle; consistent time away from the caregiving role, however brief; support from a partner that goes beyond task sharing to include genuine emotional acknowledgment; and professional support when anxiety is significantly impairing — from a therapist, from a postpartum support group, or from a psychiatrist when medication is indicated.

The cultural message that asking for help represents inadequacy is both false and harmful. Mothers who receive genuine support are better regulated, more available to their children, and more effective caregivers than mothers who are depleted. Asking for and accepting support is not a sign of inadequacy — it is one of the most competent things a mother can do.

Exercise: The Good Enough Mother

Write a description of a "good enough" mother — not a perfect one, but one who is genuinely adequate. Include: the mistakes she makes, the things she does not do, the ways her children experience her imperfection and are unharmed by it. Compare this description to the standard you actually hold yourself to. Notice the gap. The gap between good enough and the standard you hold yourself to is the source of a significant portion of your maternal anxiety.

Key Takeaways

- Maternal anxiety is one of the most common and least discussed experiences of motherhood — stigma keeps it private and untreated far longer than necessary.
- The invisible mental load — the cognitive and emotional labor of tracking family needs — creates chronic vigilance that is physiologically exhausting and anxiety-maintaining.
- Intrusive thoughts about harm coming to a baby are extremely common and are not predictive of behavior — they are a feature of anxious hypervigilance, not danger.
- The perfectionism of modern intensive parenting creates a guaranteed gap between standard and reality that is itself anxiety-generating.
- Reducing maternal anxiety requires both cognitive work — addressing catastrophic thoughts and shame — and structural work — making the mental load visible and redistributing it.

CHAPTER 9

Social Anxiety and the Pressure to Perform

Social anxiety — the fear of negative evaluation in social situations — is the third most common mental health condition in the world and is significantly more prevalent in women. While biological factors play a role, the social dimension of women's social anxiety is particularly important: women face a set of social expectations — to be warm, competent, attractive, likable, not too aggressive but not too passive — that creates a performance pressure that is inherently anxiety-generating.

The most cognitively costly aspect of this pressure is the self-monitoring it requires. Women who are socially anxious — and many who are not — maintain a running internal commentary on their social performance: how they are coming across, whether they said the right thing, whether others are responding positively, whether they have talked too much or too little, whether their appearance is acceptable. This monitoring is exhausting, it impairs the very performance it is designed to protect, and it prevents the genuine connection that is the actual goal of social interaction.

The Social Expectations Women Navigate

The social expectations that women navigate are genuinely contradictory, and the anxiety this creates is not simply a cognitive distortion — it reflects a real social reality. Women are expected to be warm and personable but not girlish, competent and authoritative but not aggressive, physically attractive but not vain about it, available and accommodating but not a pushover. These standards apply simultaneously and shift depending on context, requiring a level of continuous calibration that is itself cognitively demanding and anxiety-generating.

The penalty for getting this calibration wrong is real. Research consistently shows that women who are perceived as too assertive are rated as less likable, women who are perceived as too accommodating are rated as less competent, and women who deviate significantly from appearance norms face social and professional consequences that men in comparable situations do not. The anxiety of social performance in women is not imaginary — it reflects a genuine double bind that makes the navigation of social situations genuinely harder.

The Self-Focused Attention Problem

Social anxiety is maintained primarily by self-focused attention — the direction of cognitive resources inward, toward monitoring your own performance, rather than outward, toward the social situation. This creates a vicious cycle: self-focused attention impairs social performance (because cognitive resources are not available for genuine engagement), the impaired performance confirms the feared negative evaluation, and the fear of negative evaluation increases self-focused attention.

The treatment implication is counterintuitive: the solution to social anxiety is not to prepare more thoroughly or monitor your performance more carefully. It is to direct attention outward — toward the people you are with, toward the conversation, toward genuine interest in others' experience — and to allow the social interaction to unfold without internal commentary.

Post-Event Processing

One of the most distinctive features of social anxiety is post-event processing — the tendency to review social interactions after they have ended, looking for evidence of failure, replaying moments that felt awkward, and constructing increasingly negative assessments of how the interaction went. This processing is not helpful and is not problem-solving: it reliably produces a more negative assessment of the event than the contemporaneous experience, and it maintains the anxious state long after the social situation has passed.

Post-event processing is driven by a mismatch between how the socially anxious person experiences the interaction from the inside — as a performance ridden with errors and judgment — and how others experience it from the outside. Research consistently shows that socially anxious people are significantly more critical of their own social performance than observers are, and that the errors they believe they committed are largely invisible to others. But because the processing uses internally generated data (how it felt) rather than externally available data (how others actually responded), it produces conclusions that are more negative than the evidence supports.

The Role of Preparation in Social Anxiety

Preparation for social situations is a double-edged tool for socially anxious women. Some preparation is genuinely helpful — knowing the context of an event, having a few conversation topics in mind. But the over-preparation that anxiety drives — rehearsing conversations in detail, anticipating every possible scenario — is a safety behavior that maintains social anxiety rather than reducing it.

The specific problem with over-preparation is that it focuses attention inward — on your own performance and management of the situation — rather than on genuine social engagement. It also confirms the anxious belief that you are not capable of handling social situations without extensive management, reinforcing the underlying anxiety.

The threshold for adequate preparation varies by situation: knowing what the event is and the social context usually is sufficient. When you notice that your pre-event preparation is generating anxiety rather than confidence, that is a signal that preparation has crossed into safety behavior and is maintaining rather than managing anxiety.

Building Social Confidence

The evidence-based treatments for social anxiety include exposure — the deliberate approach of avoided social situations — combined with attention training to redirect focus outward, and the cognitive restructuring of catastrophic social predictions. The key principle is approach over avoidance: every social situation approached rather than avoided is a piece of evidence that challenges the anxious prediction and builds the confidence that avoidance prevents from developing.

Graduated exposure — beginning with lower-anxiety social situations and gradually working toward higher-anxiety ones — is more effective than attempting to immediately approach the most frightening situations. The goal of each exposure is not to have a perfect social experience but to complete the exposure and discover that the feared catastrophe did not occur. Over time, the brain's threat assessment of social situations updates, and the anxiety response diminishes.

Exercise: Attention Training

In your next social interaction, make a deliberate experiment: for the first few minutes, notice how much of your attention is directed inward (monitoring yourself) versus outward (genuinely attending to the other person). Then deliberately shift your attention fully outward: focus entirely on what the other person is saying, what their face and tone communicate, what questions their words raise for you. Notice whether the quality of the interaction changes when your attention is fully outward.

Social Media and Women's Social Anxiety

Social media has created a new dimension of social anxiety that the existing research literature was not designed to address: the perpetual availability of social comparison, the visibility of social exclusion, the ambiguous signals of digital interaction, and the performance demands of a public-facing digital identity. For women with social anxiety, social media amplifies many of the core patterns: the self-conscious self-presentation, the monitoring of others' responses, the comparison of self to others, and the interpretation of ambiguous signals as negative.

The research on social media and well-being consistently shows that passive social media use — scrolling and consuming without active engagement — is associated with increased anxiety and reduced well-being, while active social media use — posting, commenting, connecting — has more neutral or positive effects. The particularly damaging pattern is social comparison: comparing your unfiltered inner experience to the curated public presentation of others' lives.

Managing social media in the context of social anxiety requires a realistic assessment of how digital social interaction affects your anxiety: does it amplify monitoring and comparison? Does it provide a substitute for in-person connection that feels safer in the short term but maintains avoidance? Does it create additional sources of ambiguous signals that fuel relationship anxiety? An honest assessment may point toward reducing or restructuring social media use as a meaningful anxiety intervention.

The Recovery from Social Anxiety: What Progress Looks Like

Progress in social anxiety recovery does not look like the elimination of social anxiety. It looks like a gradual reduction in the intensity of anxiety in social situations; the ability to engage with social situations that were previously avoided; the reduction of post-event processing time and intensity; and the growing confidence that anxiety in social situations is manageable rather than catastrophic.

The milestones of social anxiety recovery are behavioral rather than emotional: attending the social event even when anxious, rather than declining because anxious; speaking in the meeting even when anxious, rather than staying silent; initiating contact even when anxious about the response, rather than waiting to be contacted. These behavioral milestones precede the emotional ones — the reduced anxiety typically follows the changed behavior, not the other way around.

This is one of the most important insights of behavioral anxiety treatment: you do not need to feel less anxious before you can change your behavior. You change your behavior — approach rather than avoid — and the anxiety follows, because the behavior change provides the evidence that the anxious prediction was wrong. Waiting to feel less anxious before engaging more is the trap that maintains social anxiety indefinitely.

Exercise: Post-Event Challenge

After your next social interaction that triggers post-event processing, make a deliberate practice: (1) Write down your internal assessment of how the interaction went. (2) Write down only the external evidence — what actually happened, what others actually said and did. (3) Compare the two. Notice whether your internal assessment is supported by the external evidence or whether it has diverged in a more negative direction. (4) Write a more evidence-based assessment. Practice this every time post-event processing begins.

The Physical Experience of Social Anxiety in Women

Social anxiety has a pronounced physiological component that is particularly important to understand because it creates a feedback loop that amplifies the anxiety. When social anxiety is activated, the body responds: heart rate increases, skin flushes, voice may tremble, hands may shake. These physical responses are then noticed by the anxious person — and interpreted as additional evidence of social failure. "Everyone can see I'm blushing. They can see I'm nervous. Now they know I'm not as confident as I should be."

This interpretation adds a second layer of anxiety on top of the first, producing the experience that many socially anxious women describe as their worst fear materializing: the anxiety becoming visible. The irony is that the physical symptoms of social anxiety are typically far less visible to others than they feel from the inside. Research consistently shows that socially anxious people overestimate how visible their anxiety symptoms are to others — a phenomenon called the *illusion of transparency*.

Understanding the illusion of transparency is genuinely relieving for many women with social anxiety. Your blush is almost certainly less visible than it feels. The tremor in your voice that you are acutely aware of is generally not perceptible to listeners. The racing heart and shallow breathing that feel overwhelming internally do not broadcast externally. Working with this information — deliberately reminding yourself that what you feel is not what others see — reduces the second-layer anxiety that the physical symptoms generate.

The somatic regulation tools of Chapter 7 have a specific role here: applied immediately before social situations, they reduce the physiological activation to a level that makes the anxiety less visible and less distracting. The physiological sigh — the double inhale followed by a long exhale — is particularly useful in the moments before a social interaction because it can be done unobtrusively and produces a rapid reduction in sympathetic nervous system activation.

Social Anxiety and Technology: The Double-Edged Digital World

Technology has changed the landscape of social anxiety in ways that are both relieving and complicating. On the relieving side: text-based communication, email, and messaging remove many of the immediate-response demands of face-to-face interaction, giving socially anxious people more control over their communication and more time to construct responses. Many socially anxious women report feeling genuinely more competent and confident in written communication than in real-time interaction.

The complicating side is significant. Beyond the comparison dynamics described earlier in this chapter, social media adds a mechanism of its own. The constant low-level monitoring of how posts are received — how many likes, what comments, whether silence means disapproval — is a form of ongoing reassurance-seeking that maintains social anxiety rather than reducing it.

Text-based communication, while less immediately demanding, also introduces its own social anxiety — the anxiety of ambiguous silence. When a text goes unanswered, the anxious mind fills the silence with catastrophic interpretation. When an email receives a brief response to a detailed communication, the interpretation tends toward negative rather than neutral. Managing text-based social anxiety requires the same cognitive restructuring as face-to-face social anxiety: identifying the evidence for multiple interpretations rather than defaulting to the most negative one.

A useful practice for technology-driven social anxiety is to set deliberate limits on monitoring: checking social media at specific times rather than continuously, giving email responses a realistic window rather than interpreting delay as rejection, and practicing tolerating the ambiguity of digital silence without immediately seeking clarity. These limits reduce the cognitive load of ongoing monitoring and interrupt the reassurance-seeking cycle that technology makes so accessible.

Counter-Evidence: How Social Confidence Accumulates

Approaching avoided social situations gives the brain the opportunity to update its threat assessment — but that update is not automatic. Whether repeated approach accumulates into genuine confidence depends on what you do with the evidence each approach produces.

The key phrase is "the opportunity to update." The update only happens if you allow yourself to process what actually occurred rather than defaulting to post-event processing that emphasizes what went wrong. After a social interaction, deliberately ask: What actually happened? What went well? What evidence do I have that the interaction was as bad as my anxiety predicted? The practice of counter-evidence gathering is what allows the brain's threat assessment to update rather than confirming the same negative prediction each time.

Social confidence also builds through the accumulation of competent social moments — conversations that went well, connections that were genuine, moments of being seen and valued by others. Anxious people tend to discount these moments and weight negative moments more heavily. Deliberately attending to positive social experiences — noticing them, recording them, allowing them to matter — is a counter to the negativity bias that social anxiety amplifies.

Exercise: The Social Evidence Record

For the next two weeks, after every significant social interaction, write down three things: (1) What the anxiety predicted would happen. (2) What actually happened. (3) One moment from the interaction that went well. Review the record at the end of two weeks. Do the anxiety's predictions match the actual outcomes? Is there a gap between what is predicted and what occurs? This record builds the evidence base for challenging the social anxiety narrative and tracking the accumulation of genuine social competence.

Key Takeaways

- Social anxiety in women reflects both the biological vulnerability to social threat evaluation and the genuine social double bind that makes social performance harder for women.
- Social anxiety is maintained primarily by self-focused attention — cognitive resources directed inward toward performance monitoring rather than outward toward genuine engagement.
- Post-event processing — reviewing social interactions for evidence of failure — produces more negative assessments than the actual evidence supports and maintains anxiety between social situations.
- The solution is not better performance monitoring but directed attention outward and systematic approach of avoided social situations.

CHAPTER 10

Building Long-Term Resilience: The Four Pillars

Managing anxiety is not only about intervening when anxiety is high. It is about building a life and a nervous system that is less vulnerable to anxiety in the first place — a structurally lower baseline of threat-readiness that makes the tools of the previous chapters less necessary because the system is less activated to begin with.

Research on anxiety resilience consistently identifies four lifestyle factors that have the strongest impact on baseline anxiety: sleep, physical movement, nutrition, and social connection. These are not soft add-ons to the real work of anxiety management. They are the physiological foundation on which every cognitive and somatic tool depends.

Pillar One: Sleep

Sleep deprivation and anxiety have a bidirectional relationship that creates one of the most vicious cycles in mental health. Anxiety disrupts sleep — through hyperactivation, rumination, and the physiological arousal that makes it difficult to fall or stay asleep. And sleep deprivation amplifies anxiety — by increasing amygdala reactivity, reducing prefrontal cortex regulation, and elevating cortisol.

The specific sleep architecture most relevant to anxiety is slow-wave sleep and REM sleep — the two stages in which emotional processing and physiological restoration occur. These are the stages most disrupted by anxiety and most important for anxiety recovery. The research on sleep and anxiety is unambiguous: prioritizing sleep is not a luxury, it is an anxiety intervention.

For women, the hormonal relationship with sleep adds additional complexity. Progesterone has sedating effects — its decline in the premenstrual phase can disrupt sleep. Estrogen decline in perimenopause is the primary driver of night sweats, which fragment sleep and produce the daytime fatigue and cognitive impairment that compound anxiety. Addressing hormonal sleep disruption may require medical attention in addition to behavioral sleep interventions.

The most evidence-based sleep intervention for anxiety-related sleep disruption is Cognitive Behavioral Therapy for Insomnia. The basics: maintain a consistent wake time regardless of how poorly you slept; use the bed only for sleep; get out of bed if you have been awake for more than 20 minutes;

and avoid the compensatory behaviors — napping, extending sleep time, going to bed earlier — that perpetuate insomnia.

Pillar Two: Physical Movement

The evidence for exercise as an anxiety intervention is strong and consistent. Regular aerobic exercise — at a moderate intensity, for at least 30 minutes, at least three times per week — produces anxiolytic effects comparable to medication for mild to moderate anxiety. The mechanisms include: metabolizing stress hormones, increasing GABA and serotonin, reducing amygdala reactivity, and building the sense of physical capability that translates into psychological resilience.

For women, the hormonal interaction with exercise adds an additional layer of benefit: exercise helps regulate cortisol and supports estrogen metabolism in ways that reduce the hormonal amplification of anxiety described in Chapter 2. Strength training in particular has been shown to reduce anxiety symptoms and improve body image in women — an important consideration given the relationship between body image concerns and anxiety in women.

The barrier to exercise for many anxious women is not knowledge but implementation: the very symptoms of anxiety — fatigue, low motivation, self-critical thinking — make it harder to begin and sustain exercise habits. Starting with small, achievable commitments — a 10-minute daily walk rather than a commitment to the gym three times a week — is more likely to build the habit than ambitious goals that collapse under the weight of anxiety.

Pillar Three: Nutrition

The gut-brain axis — the bidirectional communication pathway between the gut microbiome and the brain — is increasingly recognized as a significant factor in anxiety. The gut produces roughly 95% of the body's serotonin — though that serotonin acts locally on digestion and does not cross into the brain, so it is not the same pool that regulates mood. The gut-brain connection that matters for anxiety runs through other routes: vagal signaling, immune pathways, and the metabolites that gut bacteria produce, all of which the diversity and health of the microbiome influence, along with the stress response.

The nutritional approaches most consistently linked to reduced anxiety include: a diverse diet rich in plants and fermented foods to support microbiome diversity; adequate protein intake to support neurotransmitter production; omega-3 fatty acids from oily fish or supplementation, which have anti-inflammatory and anxiolytic effects; and the reduction of caffeine and alcohol, both of which directly amplify anxiety — caffeine by stimulating the sympathetic nervous system, alcohol by disrupting sleep architecture and creating rebound anxiety.

Blood sugar stability deserves particular mention for women with anxiety. Hypoglycemia — low blood sugar — produces physical symptoms that are identical to anxiety: shakiness, heart pounding, sweating, cognitive impairment. For women who skip meals or eat irregularly, blood sugar dips can trigger or amplify anxiety in ways that are easily addressed through regular, balanced eating. If your anxiety reliably worsens between meals or when you have not eaten, blood sugar regulation is worth specific attention.

Pillar Four: Social Connection

Social connection is one of the most powerful regulators of the human nervous system. Co-regulation — the calming of one nervous system through contact with another calm nervous system — is a fundamental biological mechanism. The presence of a trusted other person literally changes the physiological state of the person with them, reducing cortisol, slowing heart rate, and downregulating the threat response.

For women, social connection is a particularly potent stress buffer. Research introduced the concept of *tend-and-befriend*: the observation that women under stress are more likely than men to seek social connection as a coping response, and that this response is associated with oxytocin release that directly reduces anxiety. Maintaining genuine social connection — not performative social activity but real relationships characterized by mutual trust and support — is one of the most effective long-term anxiety interventions available.

The quality of social connection matters as much as the quantity. Relationships characterized by performance, competition, or chronic conflict do not provide the co-regulatory benefit of genuine connection — they add to the anxiety burden rather than reducing it. Investing in relationships where you can be honest about your experience, where vulnerability is met with empathy rather than judgment, is a direct investment in your anxiety resilience.

Exercise: Pillar Assessment

Rate each of the four pillars in your current life on a scale of 1–10. Sleep: ___. Movement: ___. Nutrition: ___. Social connection: ___. The lowest-scoring pillar is your highest-leverage target. What is one specific, realistic change you could make in that area this week? Not a complete overhaul — one change that moves the needle. Commit to that one change for two weeks before adding another.

Resilience as a Practice, Not a Trait

Resilience is sometimes presented as though it were a fixed characteristic — something you either have or do not have. The research does not support this view. Resilience is a set of practices and capacities that develop with experience and deliberate effort, and that can be built by anyone regardless of their starting point.

The practices that most consistently build resilience include: regularly doing things that are difficult and discovering that you can manage them; maintaining meaningful connections with others even when you would prefer to withdraw; finding ways to make meaning from difficult experiences rather than treating them as purely random; and maintaining a sense of agency — the belief that your actions matter — even in circumstances that feel overwhelming.

For women with anxiety, the resilience practice that is often most important is the experience of completing an anxiety-provoking situation and surviving it. Each completion updates the brain's threat assessment. Each survival is evidence against the catastrophic prediction. The accumulation of these experiences — built through the gradual approach of anxiety-triggering situations — is the mechanism by which resilience grows.

When Life Gets Hard: Maintaining Gains Under Pressure

The most common moment for anxiety management progress to reverse is when life gets genuinely hard. A major loss, a health crisis, a relationship breakdown, a significant professional setback — these events produce legitimate distress that can look, from the inside, indistinguishable from the anxiety that was being managed.

The important distinction is between situational distress — a proportionate emotional response to a difficult situation — and anxiety disorder symptoms that return in the context of the stress. Situational distress does not require the same intervention as anxiety disorder; it requires the same self-compassion, social support, and self-care as any grief or difficulty. Anxiety symptoms that return — the rumination, the avoidance, the catastrophizing — can be addressed with the same tools that worked before, even if the tools feel harder to access when life is genuinely difficult.

Maintenance during hard periods is more effective than recovery afterward. Keeping the four pillars in place during difficult periods — particularly sleep, social connection, and some form of movement — preserves the physiological baseline that makes the cognitive and behavioral tools accessible. The pillars are hardest to maintain when they are most needed. They are also most important then.

Exercise: Connection Audit

List the five people you spend the most time with, including digital contact. For each, rate: (1) Does this relationship leave you feeling more regulated or more activated? (2) Can you be honest and vulnerable in this relationship? (3) Does this person's presence calm your nervous system? The relationships that genuinely regulate you are your most important resilience resources. Are you investing in them enough?

Anxiety and the Nervous System over a Lifetime

One of the most encouraging findings from anxiety research is that the nervous system retains plasticity throughout life — the capacity to form new patterns, update threat assessments, and develop new regulatory habits does not diminish significantly with age. Women who begin addressing their anxiety in their forties, fifties, or sixties make as much genuine progress as women who begin in their twenties. The timeline of change may differ, but the capacity for change does not.

What does change with age is the context: the specific life circumstances that make anxiety more or less likely, the hormonal landscape that shapes the biology of anxiety, and the accumulated evidence — both for and against — the anxious beliefs that have organized the anxiety pattern over years. Working with longer-standing anxiety patterns requires the same tools as working with more recent ones, but often benefits from more deliberate attention to the evidence that has accumulated over a lifetime against the anxious narrative.

The four pillars are particularly important to sustain across life stages because their impact on anxiety is cumulative. The woman who has maintained good sleep habits, regular movement, a nutritionally supportive diet, and genuine social connections through her forties and fifties enters the hormonal transition of perimenopause with a significantly more resilient nervous system than the woman who has not. Building the pillars is not just a treatment for current anxiety — it is insurance for the anxious challenges that future life stages will bring.

The Ripple Effect of Your Recovery

The recovery from anxiety that you build does not stay contained to your own experience. It ripples outward through every relationship you have. The mother who is less anxious is more present with her children, more regulated in moments of their distress, more capable of the attuned co-regulation that children need for their own nervous system development. The partner who is less anxious is more emotionally available, less reassurance-seeking, more capable of genuine intimacy. The colleague who is less anxious is more collaborative, less conflict-avoidant, more able to give and receive honest feedback.

The research on intergenerational transmission of anxiety is clear: untreated parental anxiety is one of the strongest predictors of anxiety in children, through both genetic and environmental pathways. The environmental pathway — the anxious parenting behaviors, the anxious modeling of threat perception, the anxious avoidance of situations — is the one most accessible to change through the work of anxiety recovery. When you address your anxiety, you are not only reducing your own suffering. You are changing what your children learn about how to respond to uncertainty and difficulty.

None of this is meant to add pressure to an already demanding task. It is meant to acknowledge something that often goes unnamed: the work of addressing anxiety is genuinely valuable work, not just for you but for the people around you. The investment of time and effort and discomfort that anxiety recovery requires is not selfish. It is one of the most generous things you can do for the relationships that matter most to you.

Exercise: Your Anxiety Recovery Vision

Take 10 minutes to write about what your life would look like with significantly reduced anxiety. Not the complete absence of anxiety — a realistic vision of a life in which anxiety is not limiting your choices, consuming your energy, or preventing genuine engagement with what matters most to you. Be specific: what would you do differently? What relationships would look different? What opportunities would you approach that anxiety currently prevents? This vision is not wishful thinking — it is the destination that the practices in this book are designed to help you reach.

Key Takeaways

- The four pillars of anxiety resilience — sleep, movement, nutrition, and social connection — are the physiological foundation on which all anxiety management tools depend.
- Sleep deprivation and anxiety are bidirectionally linked; hormonal disruption compounds sleep challenges for women, requiring both behavioral and sometimes medical attention.
- Regular aerobic exercise produces anxiolytic effects comparable to medication for mild to moderate anxiety; starting small increases the likelihood of sustaining the habit.
- Blood sugar stability — through regular, balanced eating — can significantly reduce anxiety in women whose anxiety is amplified by hypoglycemic episodes.
- Genuine social connection — the kind involving mutual trust, vulnerability, and support — directly regulates the nervous system and is one of the most potent anxiety buffers available.

CHAPTER 11

Anxiety at Work: Navigating Professional Anxiety in Women

The workplace is one of the most consistent sources of anxiety for women, for reasons that are both individual and structural. Individual anxiety patterns — imposter syndrome, social anxiety, perfectionism, people-pleasing — manifest in professional settings in specific ways that create particular challenges. And structural factors — gender dynamics, underrepresentation, the double bind of professional women's behavior expectations — create a genuinely more anxiety-generating environment for women than for men in equivalent roles.

Understanding both dimensions is important. Individual anxiety patterns are addressable through the tools in this book. Structural factors require a different kind of response — one that involves accurate perception of a real situation rather than cognitive restructuring of a distorted one. The goal is not to CBT your way into accepting a genuinely inequitable work environment, but to have clear enough perception to distinguish between what is anxiety-distortion and what is accurate reality, and to respond to each appropriately.

The Workplace Manifestations of Imposter Syndrome

In the workplace, imposter syndrome typically produces a set of behaviors that are immediately recognizable: staying in the background in meetings despite having relevant expertise; over-preparing for presentations to a degree that costs more time than it returns; deferring to others' opinions even when your own assessment is more accurate; avoiding asking for a raise or promotion because you do not feel ready enough; and accepting credit for work reluctantly or attributing success to the team, the luck, the favorable circumstances — to anything except your own competence.

Each of these behaviors has a real cost. The woman who stays in the background in meetings is not developing her professional voice or building the organizational visibility that supports advancement. The woman who defers to others' assessments is not developing the confidence in her own judgment that comes from making decisions and observing their outcomes. The woman who does not ask for the raise she has earned is not progressing at the rate her contributions merit.

The intervention for workplace imposter syndrome is the same as for imposter syndrome generally — the evidence audit, the defusion from fraud thoughts, the approach of avoided professional challenges — with the addition of tracking professional outcomes explicitly. Women with imposter syndrome often have genuinely better data than they allow themselves to use: positive performance reviews that were dismissed, successful projects that were attributed to luck, feedback that was discounted. Creating a deliberate record of professional accomplishments and outcomes provides evidence that is harder to dismiss than general self-assessment.

Assertiveness and the Double Bind

Assertiveness in the workplace is a particular challenge for women because of the gender double bind: assertive behavior that is valued and expected in men is evaluated negatively when displayed by women. Women who are direct, who advocate for themselves and their ideas, who take up space in conversations, are more likely to be described as aggressive, difficult, or unlikable than men who display identical behavior.

This creates a genuine dilemma, and it is important to be honest about it. The advice to simply be more assertive, while accurate as far as it goes, does not acknowledge the real penalty that many women pay for assertiveness in certain environments. The calibration required — being direct enough to be effective, not so direct as to trigger the penalty — is genuinely difficult and genuinely anxiety-generating.

The approach that research supports is strategic assertiveness: identifying the contexts, relationships, and moments where assertiveness is most likely to be effective and least likely to trigger the double-bind penalty; building a track record of competence and collegiality that provides relational credit to draw on when you are assertive; and finding allies — male and female — who can amplify your ideas and advocacy in settings where direct advocacy from you might backfire.

Managing Anxiety Around Performance Reviews and Feedback

Performance reviews and critical feedback are reliable anxiety triggers for most anxious women, often to a degree that is disproportionate to the actual stakes. The anxiety begins well before the review, as rumination about potential criticisms competes with ongoing work. It intensifies in the moment, often impairing the ability to engage with the feedback calmly and clearly. And it can continue long after, as negative feedback is replayed and amplified while positive feedback is discounted.

The CBT approach to performance review anxiety focuses on the cognitive distortions that amplify the stakes: catastrophizing about the consequences of any negative feedback; mind-reading the reviewer's assessment before receiving it; all-or-nothing thinking that turns a mixed review into a total failure. Cognitive restructuring before the review — deliberately identifying the evidence for a range of possible outcomes rather than only the worst — reduces the anxiety in the moment.

The somatic approach focuses on the physiological activation that impairs performance in the review itself. The techniques of Chapter 7 — extended exhale breathing, grounding

— applied immediately before the review can reduce physiological activation to a level that allows for genuine engagement with the feedback. Treating the feedback as information rather than as verdict on your worth is the reframe that makes this possible.

Boundaries at Work and the People-Pleasing Professional

People-pleasing in the workplace has specific professional consequences. The woman who cannot say no to additional requests becomes the team's default extra capacity. The woman who takes responsibility for others' mistakes to maintain harmony becomes the person others are less careful around. The woman who consistently accommodates others' schedules and priorities at the expense of her own strategic work becomes perpetually reactive rather than proactive.

Professional boundary-setting requires the same distress tolerance as personal boundary-setting, plus the specific skills of managing professional relationships in which the power dynamics are more complex than in personal relationships. Declining a request from a peer is different from declining a request from a supervisor. Expressing a differing professional opinion in a meeting requires different skills than expressing a personal preference in a friendship.

The most effective professional boundary-setting acknowledges the relationship and the request before declining: "I know this project is important and I want to support it — I'm not in a position to take it on right now because of my current commitments. Can we talk about priorities?" This approach

— acknowledge, decline clearly, offer alternatives — maintains the relationship while setting the limit and prevents the accumulation of overcommitment that is one of the primary drivers of professional burnout.

Exercise: Professional Accomplishments Record

Create a running document of your professional accomplishments — specific outcomes, positive feedback, successful projects, skills developed, problems solved. Update it monthly. When imposter syndrome tells you that you are not really competent, consult this document. The specific, concrete nature of the record is more effective against imposter syndrome than general reassurance.

Managing Anxiety in High-Pressure Work Environments

High-pressure work environments — deadline-driven, competitive, high-stakes, or characterized by significant power differentials — amplify anxiety in ways that require specific management strategies beyond the general anxiety tools. The chronic activation that these environments produce depletes the nervous system's regulatory capacity over time, making the four pillars of Chapter 10 particularly essential.

The specific challenges of high-pressure work environments for anxious women include: the difficulty of maintaining the somatic regulation practices that reduce anxiety when the environment itself is running at a pace that feels incompatible with pausing; the amplification of people-pleasing when the stakes of disapproval feel career-defining; and the way that high-pressure environments normalize overwork and under-recovery in ways that are particularly damaging for the hormonal-anxiety interaction described in Chapter 2.

Sustainable high performance — the kind that is maintained over years rather than burning out over months — requires the deliberate protection of recovery time and regulation practices even within high-pressure environments. The women who maintain genuine high performance over long careers are not the ones who sacrifice the most sleep and health, but the ones who manage their nervous system resources as carefully as they manage their professional ones.

When Anxiety Leads to Burnout

Burnout — the state of chronic exhaustion, cynicism, and reduced efficacy that results from sustained, unmanaged stress — is closely related to but distinct from anxiety. Many women with significant anxiety eventually experience burnout as a consequence of the nervous system dysregulation, sleep disruption, and chronic activation that anxiety produces when unaddressed over time.

The pathway from anxiety to burnout is often through the very coping strategies that anxiety drives: overworking (to compensate for imposter syndrome anxiety), people-pleasing (to manage relational anxiety), and perfectionistic over-preparation (to manage performance anxiety). Each of these behaviors depletes the resources — time, energy, rest, recovery — that the nervous system needs to maintain regulation.

Recovery from burnout requires addressing both the burnout symptoms and the underlying anxiety that drove the burnout-producing behaviors. Treating only the burnout without addressing the anxiety that drove it is likely to produce another burnout cycle. The tools in this book address the anxiety that underlies many burnout trajectories — but burnout itself may require additional professional support, extended rest, and structural life changes beyond the scope of anxiety management alone.

Building a Sustainable Professional Life

The goal of managing workplace anxiety is not simply to perform adequately despite anxiety. It is to build a professional life that is genuinely sustainable — one that accommodates both your professional ambitions and your nervous system's actual needs, rather than treating the nervous system as a problem to be overcome in the pursuit of professional goals.

For many ambitious women, this requires a significant reframing of the relationship between professional achievement and well-being. The cultural message is that well-being is the reward for professional achievement — something to be enjoyed when you have accomplished enough. The evidence is the opposite: well-being is the foundation of sustainable professional achievement. The most professionally effective version of yourself is the regulated, rested, connected version, not the depleted, overextended, anxious version.

Building a sustainable professional life means making decisions about work from a place of genuine values rather than anxiety-driven compulsion — taking on challenging projects because you are genuinely interested and capable, not because anxiety about appearing inadequate demands it; declining requests because the actual demands of your life make them genuinely incompatible, not because anxiety tells you that you are not capable enough to attempt them.

Exercise: One Professional Assertion

This week, identify one professional situation where you would normally defer, stay silent, or accommodate rather than advocate for your own position or needs. Practice one assertion — a question in a meeting, a request for recognition, a decline of an unreasonable request. Note the anxiety before, during, and after. Note the outcome. The gap between predicted catastrophe and actual outcome is the data that gradually changes the brain's assessment of professional assertion as threatening.

Key Takeaways

- Workplace anxiety in women reflects both individual anxiety patterns and structural factors — distinguishing between them is essential for appropriate response.
- Imposter syndrome in the workplace produces behaviors that actively limit professional advancement — tracking professional outcomes explicitly provides evidence that is harder to dismiss than general self-assessment.
- The gender double bind around assertiveness is real — strategic assertiveness, rather than wholesale assertiveness, is a more realistic and effective approach.
- Professional boundary-setting requires distress tolerance plus specific skills for managing relationships with varying power dynamics.

CHAPTER 12

Self-Compassion: The Missing Ingredient in Women's Anxiety Recovery

Self-compassion is one of the most robustly evidence-supported elements of anxiety recovery and one of the most consistently missing from women's approach to their own mental health. The same women who would respond to a friend's anxiety with warmth, understanding, and patience respond to their own anxiety with criticism, shame, and demands for better performance.

This discrepancy is not accidental. Women are socialized to extend care to others more readily than to themselves, and the self-critical internal voice that most anxious women experience is often the internalized voice of a culture that has told them their worth is contingent on performing adequately — which chronic anxiety, by definition, threatens.

What Self-Compassion Is and Is Not

Self-compassion, as defined by researcher Kristin Neff, has three components: self-kindness (treating yourself with the same warmth you would offer a friend rather than harsh self-criticism), common humanity (recognizing that suffering and imperfection are part of the shared human experience rather than signs of personal failing), and mindfulness (holding your painful experiences in balanced awareness rather than suppressing them or over-identifying with them).

Self-compassion is not self-pity, self-indulgence, or lowered standards. The research is clear on this: people who are more self-compassionate are not less motivated, less conscientious, or less likely to take responsibility for their mistakes. They are, however, more resilient in the face of failure, more willing to try difficult things because failure is less catastrophic, and more capable of learning from mistakes rather than just suffering from them.

For anxious women, self-compassion is particularly important because it directly addresses the secondary anxiety — the shame and self-criticism that layer on top of the primary anxiety experience. When you experience anxiety and then criticize yourself for experiencing anxiety ("I should be able to handle this," "Why can't I just calm down?"), you add a stress response on top of a stress response. Self-compassion interrupts this amplification loop.

The Self-Compassion Break

One of the most practical self-compassion techniques is the self-compassion break, developed by Neff and her colleagues. When you notice anxiety or suffering, pause and work through three steps: acknowledge the suffering ("This is hard. I am struggling right now."); recognize the common humanity ("Many people experience this. I am not alone in this."); and offer yourself kindness ("May I be kind to myself right now. May I give myself what I need.").

This three-step sequence directly addresses the isolation that suffering creates — the sense that you are the only one struggling, that your experience is uniquely shameful — and replaces self-critical judgment with the warm, wise response you would offer a friend. The physiological effects of this practice are measurable: self-compassion activates the care system (associated with oxytocin and endorphins) rather than the threat system, producing calming rather than additional activation.

Self-Compassion and People-Pleasing

Self-compassion has a specific role in the recovery from people-pleasing that deserves attention. The fear of disappointing others — which drives people-pleasing — is often accompanied by a belief that you should be able to meet others' needs without limit. Self-compassion challenges this belief not through assertion but through the recognition that your needs are as legitimate as others' needs, that you cannot give from an empty cup, and that caring for yourself is not selfish — it is the foundation of being able to genuinely care for others.

The woman who consistently depletes herself to meet others' needs is not, ultimately, a more generous or caring person than the woman who maintains her own well-being and gives from that sustainable place. She is a more anxious person, a more resentful person, and over time, a less capable person. Self-compassion supports the limits that protect sustainable care.

Building a Self-Compassion Practice

Self-compassion is not a natural response for most anxious women — it requires deliberate practice to override the default self-critical response. The most effective way to build a self-compassion practice is to begin with the self-compassion break, applied consistently to moments of anxiety, failure, or difficulty.

Loving-kindness meditation — the deliberate cultivation of warmth toward oneself and others — is a more formal practice that develops the self-compassion disposition more broadly. Beginning with sending warmth to others (which is typically easier) and gradually extending it to yourself is more effective than attempting to begin with self-directed kindness.

Writing exercises — writing a letter to yourself from the perspective of a compassionate friend who knows your situation fully, or describing your difficult experience in the third person ("She is struggling with anxiety and feeling ashamed of it...") — can help develop the compassionate perspective by creating the same distance that the self-compassion break achieves through language.

Exercise: The Compassionate Friend Letter

Think of the aspect of your anxiety that you find most difficult to accept or most shameful. Now write a letter from the perspective of an imaginary friend who is deeply compassionate, wise, and who knows your full situation. What would this friend say to you about your anxiety? What understanding would they offer? What kindness? Read the letter back to yourself. Notice whether you can receive this compassion as a reader that you could not offer yourself as a writer.

Self-Compassion in Relationships

Self-compassion is not only an individual practice — it changes how you relate to others. When you are able to hold your own imperfection with kindness rather than shame, you are better able to hold others' imperfection with the same quality. The inner critic that attacks you tends also to attack others, often more subtly. The self-compassion that softens the inner critic creates more genuine acceptance of the people in your life.

In the context of anxiety, the most important relational dimension of self-compassion is its role in reducing the anxious pursuit of others' approval. When your sense of worth is not contingent on others' positive evaluation — when you can offer yourself the acceptance you have been seeking from others — the urgency of people-pleasing and reassurance-seeking diminishes. Not completely, and not immediately. But meaningfully, over time.

The Inner Critic and Its Origins

Most anxious women have a highly developed inner critic — a harsh internal voice that evaluates performance, predicts failure, and punishes imperfection. Understanding this voice, rather than simply trying to silence it, is more effective for long-term change. The inner critic developed for a reason — typically as an adaptive response to early experiences in which being good enough, staying small, or anticipating criticism felt important for safety or belonging.

The inner critic is not an enemy. It is an outdated protective mechanism — one that was trying to keep you safe and that has generalized to situations where its harsh standards are no longer useful. Approaching it with curiosity rather than battle — "What is this voice trying to protect me from? What does it think will happen if it relaxes?" — often reveals the anxious core beneath the criticism and makes it possible to address that core directly rather than just trying to shut the voice down.

Identifying the inner critic's characteristic statements and recognizing them as thoughts rather than truth is a defusion practice: "There's the voice that says I'm not good enough. I notice it is here again. I don't have to believe it or act on it." Over time, this recognition reduces the inner critic's power —

not by arguing it into silence, but by developing the perspective from which it can be observed without being obeyed.

Self-Compassion and Recovery from Setbacks

The moment after a setback — a failed presentation, a relationship difficulty, a parenting moment you regret, an anxiety episode that felt out of control — is the moment when self-compassion is most needed and most difficult to access. The default response to setbacks for most anxious women is a flood of self-critical analysis: what went wrong, what should have been done differently, what this reveals about your fundamental inadequacy.

The self-compassion response to setbacks is qualitatively different: acknowledge the difficulty and the pain of what happened; recognize it as part of shared human experience rather than personal failing; and offer yourself the kindness you would offer a friend who had the same experience. This response does not eliminate the learning from the setback — self-compassion does not protect against accountability. It creates the emotional safety in which genuine learning is possible, because learning requires the honesty about what went wrong that shame makes impossible.

Women who approach their setbacks with self-compassion rather than self-criticism learn from them more effectively, recover their sense of agency more quickly, and are more willing to try again. The harsh inner critic does not improve performance by making the stakes feel higher. It impairs performance by creating the physiological and cognitive conditions of anxiety that compromise the very capacities it demands.

Exercise: Daily Self-Compassion Check-In

At the end of each day for two weeks, spend three minutes with these questions: (1) What was difficult today? (2) How did I respond to my own difficulty — with kindness or with criticism? (3) What would I say to a friend who had the same experience? (4) Can I offer myself that response now? This brief practice builds the self-compassion habit by making the contrast between self-criticism and self-compassion visible daily.

Key Takeaways

- Self-compassion — treating yourself with the same warmth you would offer a friend — directly addresses the secondary anxiety that shame and self-criticism add to primary anxiety.
- Self-compassion is not self-pity or lowered standards; research shows more self-compassionate people are more resilient and more willing to take on challenges.
- The self-compassion break — acknowledging suffering, recognizing common humanity, offering kindness — can be practiced in any moment of difficulty.
- Self-compassion supports the limits that protect sustainable care — it is the foundation of being able to genuinely care for others without depleting yourself.

BONUS CHAPTER

Anxiety in Relationships: When Your Partner Does Not Understand

One of the most isolating aspects of anxiety is experiencing it with a partner who does not share it — or who expresses it so differently that your experience feels foreign and incomprehensible to them. Partners with low anxiety often respond to anxious partners in ways that, despite being well-intentioned, make the anxiety worse: dismissing the concern, offering immediate solutions before the anxious person feels heard, or expressing frustration that the anxiety is not responding to logical reassurance.

The Well-Intentioned Responses That Do Not Help

When a partner is anxious, nonanxious partners typically respond in one of three ways, all of which are well-intentioned and none of which address what the anxious person actually needs. The first is reassurance: "It's going to be fine," "You're worrying about nothing," "That's very unlikely to happen." Reassurance provides brief relief but maintains anxiety over time by reinforcing reassurance-seeking as the primary coping strategy and by missing the underlying need to feel understood.

The second is problem-solving: "Here's what you should do about it," "Have you tried..." Well-intentioned problem-solving assumes that the anxious person has not thought of the obvious solutions, and it redirects toward the cognitive domain when the primary need is emotional regulation and co-regulation. Problem-solving is appropriate once the person feels heard and regulated — not before.

The third is frustration: "You always do this," "Can't you just relax?" "I've told you it's fine." The frustration of nonanxious partners is understandable — living with anxiety that does not respond to reassurance or logic is genuinely difficult. But expressed frustration adds relationship anxiety to the original anxiety, compounding rather than reducing the anxious person's distress.

What Anxious Partners Actually Need

Research on emotion coaching and co-regulation identifies what anxious people most need from partners: first, to feel heard and understood before any problem-solving or reassurance happens; second, to feel safe expressing anxiety without fear of judgment or dismissal; and third, to receive genuine co-regulation — the calming presence that a calm, attuned partner provides simply by being present and connected.

The most powerful thing a nonanxious partner can do when anxiety is high is simply to be present: to sit with the anxious person, to maintain physical contact if that is welcomed, to use a calm and steady voice, and to reflect back what they are hearing without judgment. "That sounds really scary" is more helpful than "It's not actually scary." "I hear that you're worried about this" is more helpful than "You don't need to worry about this."

Educating Your Partner About Anxiety

The most useful conversation you can have with a nonanxious partner about anxiety is not in the middle of an anxious episode. It is in a calm moment, when both of you are resourced. The conversation has three parts: explaining what anxiety actually feels like from the inside (including the physiological component that is not voluntary); explaining what helps and what does not; and making a specific request about what you need when anxiety is high.

The specific request is the most important part. "I need you to understand my anxiety" is not actionable. "When I'm anxious and I tell you what I'm worried about, I need you to listen without immediately telling me I'm wrong or offering solutions — can you just say something like I hear you and I'm with you first?" is actionable. The more specific you can be about what genuinely helps, the more your partner can provide it.

When Anxiety Affects the Relationship

Anxiety can affect relationships in ways that go beyond the partner's response to anxious episodes. Avoidance driven by anxiety can limit shared activities. Reassurance-seeking can create an emotional burden that builds over time. The hypervigilance of anxious attachment can create a monitoring of the relationship that the partner experiences as controlling or mistrustful. And the emotional exhaustion of chronic anxiety can reduce the capacity for the relational engagement that keeps connections alive.

Addressing these relational consequences of anxiety requires honesty — with yourself about how your anxiety is affecting the relationship, and with your partner about what is happening and why. Couples therapy can be valuable when anxiety has significantly affected the relationship: a skilled couples therapist can help both partners understand the anxiety and its relational consequences, develop communication patterns that support rather than maintain the anxiety, and rebuild the connection that anxiety may have strained.

Exercise: The Partner Conversation

Prepare for a calm conversation with your partner about anxiety by writing answers to: (1) What does anxiety feel like for me — what is the physical and mental experience? (2) What do you do that helps, even if unintentionally? (3) What do you do that makes it worse, even if unintentionally? (4) What is one specific thing I would like you to do differently when I am anxious? Use your written answers to guide the conversation. Ask your partner to listen without defending before you discuss together.

Anxiety and Conflict Avoidance in Relationships

One of the most significant ways anxiety affects relationships is through conflict avoidance — the reluctance to raise difficult topics, express genuine disagreement, or address interpersonal problems because the anticipated anxiety of conflict feels more threatening than the ongoing cost of avoidance. For women socialized to maintain relational harmony, conflict avoidance is both culturally reinforced and anxiety-driven, making it particularly resistant to change.

The cost of chronic conflict avoidance accumulates over time: resentments that are not expressed build; the partner who is never disagreed with does not get accurate feedback; and the woman doing the avoiding loses the capacity for genuine intimacy, because genuine intimacy requires the risk of authentic expression that conflict avoidance prevents. The relationship that feels safe because conflict is avoided often becomes one in which genuine closeness is impossible.

Addressing conflict avoidance requires the same graduated approach as addressing any other avoidance: starting with low-stakes disagreements and gradually building toward more significant ones, while using the distress tolerance tools of Chapter 7 to manage the anxiety that direct expression produces. The discovery that most low-stakes conflicts can be raised and resolved without catastrophic relational damage is the data that makes it possible to approach higher-stakes ones.

When a Partner's Response to Your Anxiety Becomes Its Own Problem

Most partners who respond unhelpfully to anxiety are doing so without awareness that their response is unhelpful. They are using the tools available to them — reassurance, logic, problem-solving — and genuinely trying to help. Education about what actually helps is usually sufficient to produce meaningful change in a willing partner.

However, some partner responses to anxiety cross a line from unhelpful to actively problematic: using anxiety as evidence that the anxious person is incapable of making good decisions; dismissing anxiety as manipulation or attention-seeking; expressing contempt rather than concern; or using the anxious person's vulnerability as a mechanism of control. These responses are not attempts to help that miss the mark

— they are problematic in themselves and require a different kind of response.

If your partner's response to your anxiety includes dismissal, contempt, or exploitation of your vulnerability, addressing this is a priority that goes beyond anxiety management. A therapist — individual or couples — can help clarify whether what you are experiencing is an unhelpful response that education can address, or something more problematic that requires a more significant relational response. Anxiety does not make you incapable of accurately perceiving your relational reality, and if your relational reality is genuinely difficult, the solution is not to manage your anxiety better but to address the relational reality directly.

Exercise: The Relationship Anxiety Inventory

Reflect on your closest relationship and answer honestly: (1) Are there topics you avoid raising because of anxiety about the response? (2) Do you seek reassurance more than feels healthy for both of you? (3) Does anxiety about the relationship itself — about your partner's feelings, about abandonment or rejection — consume significant mental space? (4) When conflict arises, what do you typically do? The answers to these questions map the intersection of your anxiety and your relationship, and indicate where the most important work is.

Anxiety Across Life Stages

Anxiety in women is not static — it changes in character, intensity, and focus across different life stages. In young adulthood, it tends to center on identity formation, social belonging, and early professional establishment. In the childbearing years, it is often amplified by hormonal changes, the demands of caregiving, and the invisible mental load. In midlife, it frequently involves the perimenopausal hormonal transition alongside the existential questions of midlife. And in later life, it can involve health anxiety, loss, and the recalibration of purpose and identity.

Understanding the stage-specific nature of anxiety allows for more targeted intervention. The anxiety of a 25-year-old establishing herself professionally calls for different emphasis than the anxiety of a 45-year-old navigating perimenopause, even if the underlying tools are similar. Throughout this book, the examples and emphasis have been calibrated to the most common female anxiety presentations across these stages — but the specific stage you are in will determine which chapters are most immediately relevant.

One constant across all life stages is the role of the four pillars: sleep, movement, nutrition, and social connection are foundational to anxiety resilience at every age, even as the specific challenges to maintaining each pillar change. A young professional managing irregular sleep around demanding work hours faces different sleep challenges than a perimenopausal woman managing night sweats. But for both, sleep quality is among the most powerful anxiety variables available to address.

Key Takeaways

- Well-intentioned partner responses — reassurance, problem-solving, and frustration — often make anxiety worse by missing the primary need to feel heard and co-regulated.
- What anxious partners most need: to feel heard before being helped, to feel safe expressing anxiety, and to receive genuine co-regulation through calm, attuned presence.
- The most useful conversation about anxiety with a partner happens in a calm moment, not in the middle of an anxious episode — and includes specific, actionable requests.
- When anxiety has significantly affected the relationship itself, couples therapy can be valuable for addressing both the anxiety and its relational consequences.

CONCLUSION

The Calm You Were Always Capable Of

Anxiety has probably been with you for a long time. It has shaped decisions, limited possibilities, consumed energy, and created suffering that you did not ask for and did not deserve. It has felt, at times, like a fixed part of who you are — something to be managed rather than changed.

But anxiety is not who you are. It is a state of your nervous system — one shaped by biology, by experience, by the specific circumstances of a female life in a world that makes particular demands of women. And because it is a state rather than an identity, it can change. Not eliminate — anxiety is part of the human threat-detection system and will always be with you in some form. But genuinely, structurally reduced. Not managed. Changed.

The evidence for this is not theoretical. It comes from decades of clinical research showing that the techniques in this book — the cognitive restructuring, the defusion, the somatic regulation, the gradual approach of avoided situations, the building of the four pillars — produce measurable, lasting changes in anxiety. The brain is plastic. The nervous system is responsive to experience. The attachment system updates. The patterns that anxiety has built over years are real, but they are also changeable.

The change is not linear. There will be periods of progress and periods where old patterns reassert themselves, usually under conditions of high stress or hormonal disruption or inadequate sleep. This is not failure. It is the nature of changing a deeply embedded system. The question is not whether you can achieve a permanent state of calm — you cannot, and nobody can. The question is whether you can build a different relationship to anxiety: one in which it is an experience you have rather than an identity you are, one in which the tools for changing your state are available to you and you use them.

The specific circumstances of being a woman in the world — the hormonal complexity, the relational demands, the social double binds, the invisible labor — are real and they matter. They are not excuses or limitations. They are the context in which you are doing this work, and they deserve to be held with compassion rather than judgment. You did not create the conditions that make anxiety more likely in women. You are doing the work of addressing them. That deserves acknowledgment.

Your Next Steps

Reading a book about anxiety — even an evidence-based one with practical exercises — is not the same as changing your relationship to anxiety. The change happens through practice: daily, consistent, imperfect practice of the techniques and approaches described here. The question of where to start is one of the most common barriers to beginning.

The most effective starting point is the chapter that speaks most directly to your most pressing current experience. If you are in a premenstrual high-anxiety week, start with the hormonal anxiety tools of Chapter 2 and the somatic regulation tools of Chapter 7. If you are struggling most with relationship anxiety right now, start with Chapter 4. If imposter syndrome is limiting your professional life most immediately, start with Chapter 5.

The most important commitment is to the four pillars of Chapter 10 — because they are the foundation on which everything else rests. A week of genuine attention to sleep, movement, nutrition, and social connection will change your baseline in ways that make every other technique more accessible and more effective. Start there if you are not sure where to start.

And return to this book. The chapters you skip today because they do not feel most relevant may be the ones you most need in six months, or when life circumstances shift. The tools here are yours as long as you use them. The calm you are building is cumulative — it grows with practice and with time, and it belongs to you.

The Work You Have Already Done

If you have read this far, you have already done something significant. You have engaged with the biology of your anxiety, the psychology of your anxiety patterns, and the social and hormonal context that shapes your specific experience of anxiety as a woman. You have encountered the tools — the cognitive restructuring, the defusion practices, the somatic techniques, the lifestyle foundations — that the evidence supports. That engagement is itself a form of approach rather than avoidance, and it matters.

The women who make the most progress with anxiety are not the ones who find the techniques easiest or who have the least severe anxiety. They are the ones who keep returning to the work — who pick up the thought record again after a difficult week, who return to the breathing practice after a month of neglecting it, who re-read the chapter on people-pleasing when the old patterns reassert themselves. Consistency over time is the mechanism of change, not perfection within a single week.

Allow yourself to acknowledge the courage that addressing anxiety requires. Anxiety is uncomfortable to sit with and uncomfortable to approach. The avoidance that anxiety drives is not weakness — it is the logical response of a nervous system that is trying to reduce its own discomfort. Choosing approach over avoidance, repeatedly, is a genuine act of courage. It deserves to be recognized as such.

Compassion for the Anxiety That Got You Here

The anxiety you are working with did not arrive without reason. It developed in response to real experiences, real circumstances, real demands. The nervous system that learned to be hypervigilant was responding to something — an environment that was genuinely unpredictable, relationships that required careful monitoring, social circumstances in which making mistakes felt costly. The anxiety was adaptive, once. It was trying to protect you.

The work of recovery is not to reject or overpower the anxiety that developed, but to update it: to help your nervous system learn that the conditions that made hypervigilance necessary are no longer present, or are not as dangerous as the anxiety assessment suggests, or can be navigated with tools that anxiety never had available to it. This is a relationship with the anxious part of yourself, not a battle against it.

Women who recover most fully from anxiety tend to develop this quality of compassionate understanding toward their anxiety: seeing it as the nervous system's attempt to protect rather than as a character flaw or a failure of self-control. This is not passivity or acceptance of limitation. It is the accurate understanding of what anxiety is and where it came from — understanding that makes it possible to work with the anxiety rather than against it.

What Full Recovery Looks Like

Full recovery from anxiety does not look like the permanent absence of anxious feelings. It looks like a changed relationship to the anxiety that does appear: noticing it rather than being consumed by it; using the tools available rather than defaulting to avoidance; returning to the present moment rather than being carried into future catastrophizing; and maintaining the commitments that matter to you regardless of what anxiety is saying in the moment.

It looks like approaching situations that used to be avoided — having the difficult conversation, applying for the promotion, speaking in the meeting, being vulnerable in a relationship — and discovering repeatedly that the outcome is better than anxiety predicted. Over time, these discoveries accumulate into a fundamentally different relationship to uncertainty: not the absence of anxiety about the unknown, but the confidence that you can handle what emerges.

Full recovery looks like a life that is lived in accordance with your values rather than organized around the avoidance of anxiety. The anxiety is still there, sometimes. But it is no longer the primary organizing principle of your choices. You have more of yourself available — more energy, more presence, more capacity for genuine engagement with the people and activities that matter — because the anxiety is consuming less.

That is what is available to you. Not through any single technique or breakthrough, but through the accumulation of practice and time and self-compassion that this book is designed to support. The calm you were always capable of is not a destination you arrive at. It is the quality of presence you build, one practice at a time, one approached situation at a time, one compassionate response to your own difficulty at a time.

FAQ

Frequently Asked Questions

Is anxiety something I will always have to manage?

Anxiety as a human experience — the capacity to feel worried, cautious, or activated by perceived threats — is part of the species. But anxiety as a chronic, impairing condition is not fixed. The techniques in this book, applied consistently, produce genuine reductions in baseline anxiety, not just better coping. The goal is not perfect calm but a relationship to anxiety that is manageable, that does not limit your life significantly, and that you have effective tools to address.

Should I be on medication for anxiety?

That is a decision to make with a qualified medical or psychiatric professional who knows your specific situation.

The research on anxiety treatment shows that the combination of medication and psychological therapy is more effective than either alone for moderate to severe anxiety. For mild to moderate anxiety, psychological approaches alone have outcomes comparable to medication, with the advantage that the skills learned do not stop working when you stop taking the medication.

My anxiety is much worse premenstrually — is that normal?

Yes. As described in Chapter 2, the sharp drop in estrogen and the fluctuations in progesterone that characterize the premenstrual phase directly reduce the brain's anxiety-buffering capacity and increase amygdala reactivity. Anxiety that is significantly worse premenstrually is called *premenstrual exacerbation of anxiety*, and it is both common and treatable. If your premenstrual anxiety is severe, discuss it specifically with your gynecologist or psychiatrist — targeted interventions are available.

I have tried therapy before and it did not help — why would this be different?

Not all therapy is equally effective for anxiety. The evidence base for anxiety specifically supports CBT and ACT — approaches that are active and skills-based, not primarily insight-oriented. If previous therapy did not include systematic exposure to avoided situations, cognitive restructuring of specific anxious thoughts, and somatic regulation techniques, it may not have addressed the mechanisms that maintain your anxiety. The techniques in this book reflect the current evidence base for anxiety specifically.

How long will it take to see results?

Research on CBT for anxiety typically shows meaningful improvement within 8–16 sessions of regular therapy, or 8–16 weeks of consistent practice of the techniques independently. Somatic techniques can produce immediate short-term relief from acute anxiety within a single practice. The four pillars produce accumulating benefits over weeks and months. The most honest answer is: meaningful change in a few weeks of consistent practice, significant change in a few months, and continuing improvement over the longer term.

Can I use this book alongside therapy?

Yes — and it is designed to be compatible with professional support. If you are working with a therapist, this book can provide additional psychoeducation and practice between sessions. Share it with your therapist if you find it useful — they can help you apply the concepts specifically to your situation.

I have health anxiety — is that different from general anxiety?

Health anxiety — excessive worry about illness, physical symptoms, or medical conditions — shares the same cognitive and behavioral mechanisms as other anxiety presentations but applies them specifically to health-related concerns. It involves catastrophic interpretation of physical symptoms, reassurance-seeking through repeated medical consultations or online symptom-checking, and avoidance of information that might confirm feared diagnoses. The same CBT and ACT tools apply — specifically, cognitive restructuring of catastrophic health interpretations and the reduction of reassurance-seeking behavior, which maintains health anxiety. If health anxiety is significantly impairing your life, working with a therapist who specializes in this area is advisable.

My anxiety started after a traumatic event — how is this different?

Anxiety that develops after a traumatic event — which may present as PTSD or acute stress disorder — has the same surface features as other anxiety but with a different mechanism: the nervous system has been specifically calibrated by the traumatic experience to be hyperalert to trauma-related cues. While some of the tools in this book are applicable — particularly the somatic regulation techniques of Chapter 7 — trauma-related anxiety benefits from specialized trauma-informed treatment such as EMDR or trauma-focused CBT, which address the traumatic memory processing that underlies the symptoms.

Can anxiety be completely cured?

The goal of anxiety treatment is not elimination but transformation: changing the relationship to anxiety so that it is not impairing, not limiting your life, and not producing suffering disproportionate to its informational value. Research on long-term outcomes from CBT and ACT for anxiety shows that most people who complete treatment maintain their gains over years, with anxiety remaining at a level that they can manage effectively. Occasional spikes — triggered by stress, hormonal shifts, or significant life events — are normal and are best addressed by returning to the tools rather than interpreting them as treatment failure.

My anxiety is affecting my children — what should I do?

This is one of the most important questions anxious mothers ask, and the answer is both reassuring and action-oriented. The reassuring part: research shows that anxious parents who are addressing their anxiety are not passing it to their children in the way that untreated anxiety is transmitted. The action-oriented part: getting support for your own anxiety is the most direct thing you can do to protect your children. Beyond that, the co-regulation tools in Chapter 7 apply to children as well as adults — a regulated parent is the most powerful regulator of an anxious child.

How do I know if my anxiety is hormonal or situational?

The most reliable way to identify a hormonal component to your anxiety is cycle tracking — monitoring your anxiety level daily alongside the day of your menstrual cycle for two full cycles. If your anxiety consistently spikes at the same phase of your cycle, particularly in the premenstrual week, and returns to a lower baseline after menstruation begins, a hormonal contribution is likely. Situational anxiety, by contrast, correlates more closely with specific events, circumstances, or periods of high external demand rather than cycling predictably with the hormonal calendar.

It is important to note that hormonal and situational anxiety are not mutually exclusive — a situational stressor that arrives during a hormonally vulnerable phase will produce more anxiety than the same stressor arriving at a hormonally stable phase. Understanding both dimensions allows for more targeted management: addressing the situation while also applying the hormonal anxiety support tools from Chapter 2.

What is the difference between anxiety and stress?

Stress is the response to a genuine external demand — a deadline, a difficult relationship situation, a significant life change. When the demand is addressed or resolved, the stress typically diminishes. Anxiety is a state that can be activated by genuine external demands but that also activates in the absence of specific external threats — through anticipation, rumination, and what-if thinking that extends the stress response beyond the actual stressor and into an imagined future.

In practice, stress and anxiety frequently occur together: a genuine stressor triggers a genuine stress response, and anxiety extends and amplifies that response into territory that the stressor itself does not justify. Managing anxiety effectively while under genuine stress requires addressing both dimensions: the external demand, with practical problem-solving and time management, and the anxiety, with the cognitive and somatic tools described in this book.

My doctor says my anxiety is just stress — should I push for a diagnosis?

A formal anxiety disorder diagnosis is not required to benefit from the tools in this book, and the distinction between clinical anxiety and significant stress is not always clear-cut. However, if your anxiety is significantly impairing your daily functioning — interfering with work, relationships, sleep, or daily activities — you deserve a thorough clinical assessment rather than a dismissive explanation.

If you feel your concerns are not being adequately addressed, seeking a second opinion from a mental health professional rather than a general practitioner is appropriate. Psychologists, psychiatrists, and licensed clinical social workers are better positioned than most general practitioners to assess and treat anxiety disorders. Advocating for your own mental health care is not being difficult — it is being your own best healthcare advocate.

Can anxiety cause physical symptoms?

Yes — and this is one of the most important things to understand about anxiety, because the physical symptoms it produces can themselves become a source of additional anxiety, particularly health anxiety. Anxiety activates the sympathetic nervous system, which produces a wide range of physical symptoms: heart palpitations, chest tightness, shortness of breath, dizziness, nausea, muscle tension, headaches, gastrointestinal disturbance, fatigue, and difficulty sleeping, among others.

These symptoms are real, physiological, and not imaginary — they are the body's stress response being activated by a nervous system in an anxious state. When physical symptoms appear and are misinterpreted as signs of physical illness rather than anxiety, a health anxiety cycle can develop: the physical symptoms of anxiety produce anxiety about having a serious illness, which increases anxiety, which increases the physical symptoms. Understanding that anxiety produces genuine physical symptoms — and learning to recognize them as such — is an important step in breaking this cycle.

APPENDIX

Tools, Trackers, and Quick-Reference Guides

Hormonal Anxiety Tracker Template

Use this daily for two full cycles to identify your hormonal anxiety pattern.

Day of cycle: ___ | Date: ___ | Anxiety level (1–10): ___ | Sleep quality (1–10): ___ | Energy level (1–10): ___ | Major stressors today: ___ | Somatic tools used: ___ | Notes: ___

Review at the end of each cycle: Which days had the highest anxiety? Does the pattern match the hormonal phases described in Chapter 2? Which interventions were most effective?

Cognitive Restructuring Quick Reference

Step 1: Write the anxious thought exactly as it appears. Step 2: Identify the cognitive distortion — catastrophizing, mind reading, fortune telling, all-or-nothing, or personalization. Step 3: Rate your belief in the thought from 0 to 100. Step 4: List the evidence that supports the thought. Step 5: List the evidence that contradicts the thought. Step 6: Write a more balanced alternative that reflects all the evidence. Step 7: Rate your belief in the original thought again.

Somatic Toolkit Quick Reference

Extended exhale breathing: Inhale 4 counts, exhale 7 counts. Repeat for 5 minutes. Best for: acute anxiety, pre-sleep, post-stress activation.

Physiological sigh: Double inhale (normal inhale plus a second short inhale), then long slow exhale. Best for: rapid acute anxiety relief.

5-4-3-2-1 grounding: Name 5 things you see, 4 you can touch, 3 you can hear, 2 you can smell, 1 you can taste. Best for: dissociation, acute panic, overwhelm.

Cold water: Splash cold water on face or hold wrists under cold water for 30 seconds. Best for: high acute activation, flooding.

Progressive muscle relaxation: Systematically tense and release each muscle group from feet to face, 5 seconds tension and 10 seconds release. Best for: chronic muscle tension, pre-sleep.

People-Pleasing Check-In

When you are about to say yes to something, pause and ask: Am I saying yes because I want to, or because I cannot tolerate the anxiety of saying no? What would happen if I said no or said what I actually need? Is the fear realistic? What does maintaining this pattern cost me? What would I tell a close friend in this situation?

Defusion Phrases

To practice defusion from anxious thoughts, use these phrases: "I notice I am having the thought that..." "My mind is telling me..." "I am noticing an anxious feeling about..." "There goes the worry about..." These phrases create distance from the thought without fighting it.

The Four Pillars Weekly Check-In

Rate each pillar weekly on a scale of 1–10 and note one thing to improve next week.

Sleep (target 7–9 hours consistently): This week: ___ / 10. One thing to improve: ___

Movement (target 30 min aerobic x 3 per week minimum): This week: ___ / 10. One thing to improve: ___

Nutrition (stable blood sugar, diverse plants, minimal caffeine and alcohol): This week: ___ / 10. One thing to improve: ___

Social connection (genuine, regulated, honest relationships): This week: ___ / 10. One thing to improve: ___

When to Seek Professional Support

Consider professional support if: your anxiety is significantly impairing your daily functioning; you are experiencing panic attacks; you are avoiding major life domains because of anxiety; you are experiencing intrusive thoughts that are significantly distressing; you are using alcohol or other substances to manage anxiety; you are experiencing symptoms of depression alongside anxiety; or the techniques in this book are not producing meaningful relief after 4–6 weeks of consistent practice.

Types of support to consider: individual therapy with a CBT or ACT-trained psychologist; a psychiatrist for medication evaluation if indicated; a gynecologist or endocrinologist if hormonal factors are significant; and group therapy or anxiety support groups, which offer the additional benefit of normalization and community.

The 30-Day Anxiety Reset Plan

Use this structure to build all four pillars and establish a daily anxiety practice. Each week adds one layer.

Week 1 — Foundation: Focus exclusively on sleep. Set a consistent bedtime and wake time seven days in a row. Eliminate screens for 30 minutes before bed. Practice extended exhale breathing for five minutes before sleep. Rate your sleep quality and morning anxiety each day.

Week 2 — Movement: Add 30 minutes of aerobic movement three times this week. Note the relationship between movement days and anxiety levels. Continue the sleep protocol from Week 1.

Week 3 — Cognitive: Begin the daily thought record from Chapter 6. Choose one recurring anxious thought and run it through the full restructuring process each day. Continue sleep and movement from previous weeks.

Week 4 — Connection: Reach out to one person in your support network for a genuine, honest conversation. Practice the self-compassion break daily. Review your anxiety ratings from the past four weeks and note what changed.

Common Anxiety Triggers for Women — Quick Reference

Hormonal triggers: premenstrual phase days 21–28, postpartum period, perimenopause transition, hormonal contraceptive changes. Management: cycle tracking, targeted somatic support on high-anxiety days, consultation with gynecologist for hormonal support if indicated.

Relational triggers: conflict or perceived conflict, abandonment cues, criticism real or perceived, social exclusion. Management: attachment pattern awareness, reassurance-seeking limits, direct communication skills.

Professional triggers: performance review, public speaking, high-stakes decisions, feedback. Management: imposter syndrome tools, pre-event somatic regulation, evidence audit.

Life transition triggers: new role, relationship change, loss, identity shift. Management: values clarification, acceptance practices, increased four-pillar support during transitions.

Physiological triggers: caffeine excess, alcohol, sleep deprivation, blood sugar instability, over-exercise. Management: lifestyle audit, reduction of identified triggers, nutritional support.

Recommended Reading and Resources

For further reading on the evidence-based approaches covered in this book, the following areas of research are particularly relevant: CBT for anxiety disorders, ACT and psychological flexibility, attachment theory and adult relationships, hormonal influences on mood and cognition, self-compassion and its clinical applications, and the neuroscience of the stress response.

If you are seeking professional support, the most effective way to find a therapist with expertise in anxiety is to ask specifically for a practitioner trained in CBT or ACT for anxiety disorders. Many mental health professional directories allow filtering by specialty and therapeutic approach. Telehealth has significantly expanded access to qualified anxiety treatment, making geographic location less of a barrier than it once was.

If you are supporting someone you love who experiences anxiety, the most useful thing you can do is educate yourself about what anxiety is and is not, practice the co-regulation skills described in the Bonus Chapter, and resist the impulse to provide reassurance in ways that maintain rather than reduce the anxiety. Your calm, attuned presence is genuinely one of the most effective anxiety interventions available.

Acknowledgments

This book stands on the foundation of an enormous body of clinical research and clinical practice. The researchers who have built the evidence base for CBT and ACT, the neuroscientists who have illuminated the biology of anxiety, the endocrinologists and women's health researchers who have documented the hormonal dimensions of female anxiety, and the attachment theorists who have mapped the relational roots of anxious experience — their work is the basis for everything that follows.

This book is dedicated to the women who experience anxiety not as a personal failing but as a comprehensible response to real circumstances — biological, psychological, and social — that make anxiety more likely in female experience. The response you have developed is not wrong. It is adaptive, given what it was responding to. The work is not to criticize that response but to build the capacity for a different one, in circumstances that increasingly allow it.

And to the women in the clinical literature — the participants in the studies, the clients in the case reports — whose anonymous experiences have built the evidence base that makes effective anxiety treatment possible: this book would not exist without them.

About the Author

Alex Z. Morgan writes evidence-based nonfiction on health, productivity, well-being, and personal development. Each book is built on the most current research available and designed to translate that research into practical, actionable frameworks that readers can apply immediately. All titles are available in ebook and paperback from major retailers.

Also by Alex Z. Morgan:

- *The Anxious Mind* — Vitality Press
- *The Healthy Habits Blueprint* — Vitality Press
- *The Gut Health Reset* — Vitality Press
- *Sleep Smarter* — Vitality Press

Did You Enjoy The Anxious Woman's Mind?

If this book helped you, I would be genuinely grateful if you took two minutes to leave an honest review. You do not need to write much — even a sentence or two makes a real difference in helping other readers find this book.

Search for the title at your preferred retailer to leave a review.

Thank you for reading. It means more than you know.

— Alex Z. Morgan

www.ingramcontent.com/pod-product-compliance
Lightning Source LLC
LaVergne TN
LVHW100731061126
851857LV00011B/484